DATA COLLECTION AND MANAGEMENT
A Practical Guide

Magda Stouthamer-Loeber
Welmoet Bok van Kammen

Applied Social Research Methods Series
Volume 39

SAGE Publications
International Educational and Professional Publisher
Thousand Oaks   London   New Delhi

For information address:

SAGE Publications, Inc.
2455 Teller Road
Thousand Oaks, California 91320
E-mail: order@sagepub.com

SAGE Publications Ltd.
6 Bonhill Street
London EC2A 4PU
United Kingdom

SAGE Publications India Pvt. Ltd.
M-32 Market
Greater Kailash I
New Delhi 110 048 India

Printed in the United States of America

Library of Congress Cataloging-in-Publication Data

Stouthamer-Loeber, Magda.
    Data collection and management: a practical guide / Magda
Stouthamer-Loeber, Welmoet Bok van Kammen.
        p.   cm. — (Applied social research methods series; v. 39)
    Includes bibliographical references and index.
    ISBN 0-8039-5656-8 (alk. paper). — ISBN 0-8039-5657-6 (pbk.:
alk. paper)
        1. Social sciences—Research. 2. Social sciences—Field work.
    I. van Kammen, Welmoet Bok. II. Title. III. Series.
    H62.S784   1995
    300′.723—dc20   95-9377

This book is printed on acid-free paper.

95 96 97 98 99 10 9 8 7 6 5 4 3 2 1

Sage Project Editor: Susan McElroy

DATA COLLECTION AND MANAGEMENT

Applied Social Research Methods Series
Volume 39

APPLIED SOCIAL RESEARCH METHODS SERIES

Contents

Preface

The mandate of social science research is to shed light on a wide variety of societal problems that may range from the development of violent crime to the effect of occupational training on welfare recipients. Because the phenomena of interest may have a low base rate (for example, relatively few violent delinquents in the general population) or a modest effect (for example, the effect of Head Start participation on later scholastic achievement), large numbers of people may have to be studied. Also, a longitudinal approach may be necessary to address questions concerning etiology and development or to examine outcomes of prevention and intervention efforts.

Studies involving large numbers of participants and/or several assessment waves are, by necessity, very expensive. Thus researchers undertaking such projects have a responsibility to ensure that they are executed as expertly as possible because errors in participant acquisition or data collection cannot be fixed easily and can seriously limit the interpretation of the results.

Managing a large study requires skills and practical experience that are usually not acquired in graduate school or gained from conducting smaller, college-based studies with the assistance of students. Also, information on how to conduct studies is rarely found in articles published in the scientific journals to which social scientists turn for substantive information in their fields. Thus it seems as if each researcher has to learn project management by trial and error. The "how to do it" part of conducting large studies is often learned the painful way or transferred, like family lore, from one researcher to another in hints, bits of advice, and anecdotes.

This book is part of a series that presents basic knowledge in many areas of applied social research methodology and aims to prepare researchers for the tasks involved in conducting social research. This volume focuses on the practical aspects of how to collect and manage data in field studies. We believe that this book will be useful for investigators and members of research teams who are conducting or planning to conduct field research, as well as for graduate students in the social sciences who are preparing for a research career.

Acknowledgments

We are grateful to Lee Robins, Joan McCord, and Beverly Cairns, who were generous with their advice when we were beginners; we are indebted to Maggie McDonald for correcting our (sometimes foreign) sentence construction. We also thank our colleagues Rolf Loeber and David Farrington, and we offer very special thanks to the past and current staff of the Pittsburgh Youth Study who have taken such pride in doing a good job.

This book is adapted from two previous publications:

Stouthamer-Loeber, M., van Kammen, W., & Loeber, R. (1992). The nuts and bolts of implementing large-scale longitudinal studies. *Violence and Victims*, 7, 63-78. Copyright © 1992 by Springer Publishing Company, Inc., New York, NY 10012. Used by permission.

Stouthamer-Loeber, M. (1993). Optimizing data quality of individual and community sources in longitudinal research. In D. P. Farrington, R. J. Sampson, & P-O. H. Wikstrom (Eds.), *Integrating individual and ecological aspects of crime* (pp. 259-278). Stockholm, Sweden: National Council for Crime Prevention. Copyright © 1993 by National Council for Crime Prevention. Used by permission.

1

Introduction

It is easy to be overwhelmed by the practical tasks that face social science researchers when studies involve many participants or repeated assessments. Even small studies require careful planning of financial and human resources and need to use well-prepared hiring and training strategies and efficient data collection and data management procedures to be successful. Size and complexity do not change the tasks that are involved in conducting a study, but the larger the study, the more pressing the need for an informational structure that allows an overview of the research activities and progress. This book is written to guide the reader through some of the tasks involved in carrying out high quality research and to convey the message that, with planning and continued care, even the most complex studies can be executed successfully.

REQUIREMENTS FOR GOOD RESEARCH

What are the requirements for good research? Two crucial skills are needed. The first concerns the ability to pose research questions of societal or theoretical importance. Second, once the problem to be investigated has been formulated, practical skills are needed to execute the research. Without the vision to delineate the important research issues, one may as well not bother to do a study. However, without a realistic plan and the proper tools to execute the study, the project may not get off the ground or may never fulfill its promise. Both relevant goals *and* a feasible plan of execution are needed. Our concern is with the second set of skills, those of executing a research project.

The skill to frame important research questions and the skill to plan and execute a study do not necessarily have to be embodied in one person, as long as both skills are represented in the research group. The two sets of skills, however, do not always happily coexist. Each is most likely to function optimally under different and almost opposite working conditions. The challenge for a research group is to simultaneously promote scientific innovation, which does not necessarily prosper under

1

tight management, and to ensure that the collection and processing of data occur in a careful, cost-efficient, and timely manner, which *does* require tight management.

Generally, studies are directed by individuals who excel in developing substantive ideas but do not necessarily have the pragmatic skills to conduct a study and manage a research team. This situation may be fostered if the research is based in an academic environment. Generally, academics are accustomed to interacting with peers and colleagues in an atmosphere where the work of one person does not directly affect the work of another (Prewitt, 1983).

It is not unusual to find research projects led by individuals who are reluctant to direct the practical affairs of a study. In managing a research project, however, a laissez-faire style may not work. There is a pressing need for continuous attention to direction, centralization, and the coordination of personnel and tasks.

In addition, within an academic environment, managing studies is often not valued as a contribution to an academic career in the same way as obtaining grants or publishing papers is valued. Therefore, extra effort will be required on the part of any academic who spends part of his or her time managing a large research project to ensure that the job receives recognition. This recognition is best negotiated with a department head at the time the proposal is being prepared for submission.

Tasks Involved in Managing a Project

Depending on the size of a project and the inclination of the investigator, the project may be managed by the investigator or by a person specifically hired for the job. The job of managing a project may also be divided into specific responsibilities handled by a number of people. Even when a study has a separate project manager, the principal investigator needs to be aware of the "business side" of the research and to realize the importance and the extent of the practical aspects of the job.

Regardless of how project management is distributed, there are three core aspects that need to be covered. These are personnel management, budget management, and data quality control.

First, the management of large studies is mainly the management of *people* and their job schedules. The schedules are often interlocking in that the time-line for one job determines when another job can be undertaken, requiring continuous planning and management of human resources. The task of the manager resembles that of an air traffic controller, keeping an eye on the positions and speeds of a number of planes that need to be woven into an errorless pattern of timely landings and takeoffs.

Second, the *costs* of data collection and data management form a very large portion of the budget of most studies (Weinberg, 1983). Staying within the budget depends, first, on careful planning of the budget and design of a study. However, even with the most careful planning, expenditures require constant monitoring, and sometimes it will be necessary to make creative adjustments in midstream.

Third, the *quality* of the research can never be better than the quality of the data that are collected. This should be a foremost concern to the researcher and, indeed, to all staff members. Maintaining high quality research requires constant vigilance at the level of sample selection, participant acquisition, data collection, data management, and analysis.

CHANGING RESEARCH CONDITIONS

The conditions under which research is executed have changed over the last 40 years. Strategies that worked a few decades ago may no longer be feasible or may have lost their effectiveness. Also, technological advances have opened new possibilities with regard to data collection and management.

A major area in which change is noticeable is the more restricted access to research participants. One reason for this limitation is the introduction of informed consent procedures (Robins, 1976). Access to certain databases that in the past could be used to select potential participants may be denied because prior consent is required. Also, the willingness of people to participate in a research study seems to have decreased over time, a trend that is possibly linked to a growing tendency to be suspicious of strangers. In addition, women, who were in many cases the respondents for surveys, have become less available because of their greater participation in the workforce. With the increase in the number of telephone surveys and telephone solicitations, people may also have become weary of answering questions. Another obstacle is the increased use of telephone answering machines, which restricts direct access to participants. For follow-up studies, the increased mobility of the population makes it more difficult to find participants for re-assessments. On the other hand, the increasing availability of electronic databases has made searching for participants easier.

Because of changes in society, certain traditional informants, like parents in the case of research on children, may no longer always be the best choice. For example, a substantial number of fathers do not live with their children and often have too little information to be useful informants on their children. Even mothers may know less about their children than the staff of the day care center or the live-in grandmother. Thus issues of participant access and selection have required ever-changing strategies over the past decades and, undoubtedly, will continue to challenge us in the future.

Another change that has affected how studies are conducted is the introduction of computers. Although mainframe computers were used initially for data storage and analysis, now fast-running personal computers are used for these same tasks and have become crucial for keeping track of participant scheduling, interviewer productivity, and the general management of a study. Personal computers have become almost as fast as their mainframe counterparts, and the availability of easy-to-use computer software for data management, report writing, desktop publishing, and other tasks has made them indispensable. Nowadays, practically all administrative, secretarial, and research staff are computer literate and can easily acquire additional skills to streamline many office and research functions. Improved data scanning procedures and the development of computer-assisted interviewing have also had an effect on how data are collected and processed. Researchers need to be aware that new electronic techniques and opportunities *open up all the time* and can be applied to improve the efficiency and quality of a study.

GOALS AND LIMITATIONS OF THE BOOK

The aim of this book is to help prepare researchers and project managers for the practical tasks involved in conducting studies. All studies have their own specific challenges with regard to the execution of the design. Most studies, however, need to deal to a greater or lesser extent with the issues raised in this volume. Some of the issues concern general principles applicable to the whole research operation, like careful planning, documentation, scrupulous honesty, and insistence on high quality. Other issues deal with specifics, such as what should be covered in the training of interviewers or how to ensure a high participation rate.

Much of what we will discuss is based on our own experience in conducting the Pittsburgh Youth Study. To understand the strengths and weaknesses of our experience, a brief outline of this project follows.

The Pittsburgh Youth Study, as part of the Program of Research on the Causes and Correlates of Delinquency (Huizinga, Loeber, & Thornberry, 1993), was designed to examine the development of prosocial and antisocial behavior in boys. The project consists of three samples, selected from students in grades 1, 4, and 7 in Pittsburgh public schools. Based on screening information, the 250 most antisocial boys in each sample were selected for follow-up together with an equal number randomly selected from the remainder. For three years these samples were followed up every 6 months. At a later stage of the study, the youngest and the oldest samples were followed up every year.

At the time of writing this book, we have prepared for and conducted 15 assessment waves, ranging in size from 500 subjects to 2300 subjects to be assessed in a 3-month period. The age of the subjects ranged, over time, from 7 to 20. Data were collected from the boys, their primary caretakers, teachers, school records, police and court records, and the U.S. Census. Interviews took place in the participants' homes.

Because initially the assessments were repeated every 6 months, we had to learn quickly to be very organized in terms of the preparation of assessment booklets; hiring, training, and supervision of interviewers; searching for participants; the distribution of questionnaires to teachers; payment of participants and interviewers; and data entry and management.

No one on our team had ever collected data on this scale and, of course, we did not foresee all the problems we encountered. Initially, we were inefficient and made errors. Very early on we decided not to waste any energy bewailing our mistakes but, rather, to learn as much as possible from them and to plan how to do things better.

Our experience sets limits to the topics discussed in this book. Although we write from the perspective of a large-scale longitudinal study conducted with an inner-city sample of families, many of the issues are also relevant for single assessment studies, studies with non-inner-city participants, evaluation studies, or smaller studies. We describe the hiring, training, and supervision of field interviewers; some of the issues discussed also apply to interviewers working in an office or to studies using telephone interviewers, mail interviews, or direct observations. Readers wishing to know more about the techniques that we do not cover are referred to Hedrick, Bickman, and Rog (1993) for selecting a research design, to Frey (1983) or Lavrakas (1993) for telephone interviewing, to Copeland and White (1991) for observations, or to the sections on mail interviews in Mangione (1995) or Miller (1991). This book does not address issues relating to qualitative assessments. For this, readers are referred to the Sage series on qualitative methods, particularly to Marshall and Rossman (1989) and other books in the series by Denzin (1989), Jorgensen (1989), and Yin (1994). A *prerequisite* for conducting a study is the availability or development of reliable and valid assessment instruments. The development of assessment instruments is an important topic that is not covered in this book; the reader is referred to Fowler and Mangione (1990) or Weller and Romney (1988) for an introduction to this area. Where appropriate, we refer readers to other works for topics outside our domain.

Overview of Chapters

Throughout the book there is an emphasis on planning and the ability to anticipate problems to ensure that the data collection and management operations run smoothly. A great deal of this planning needs to take place early in the development of the research project. In Chapter 2 we cover some of the topics that require early decisions and discuss ways to keep the budget under control. In Chapter 3 we discuss general issues related to the hiring of personnel and make suggestions for an efficient hiring process for interviewers. Chapter 4 describes an orderly set of steps to prepare for and to conduct the training of interviewers. It also discusses several ways to establish whether interviewers are ready to start interviewing. Chapter 5 offers suggestions on how to ensure high participant acquisition and retention rates. Some of the suggestions concern interviewer tactics; others deal with search methods. In Chapter 6 we advocate a vigorous program of supervision to ensure high data quality and timely data collection. We discuss how a computer-assisted tracking system can aid in the supervision of interviewers and the overall monitoring of the study. Chapter 7 covers the procedures that need to be in place to enter data and manage the assessment materials as well as the resulting computer files. The final chapter discusses a general code of conduct that should guide decisions in a research project.

2

Planning and Budget

The step-by-step planning of the actual execution of a study needs to take place at the time the study is conceptualized. Such planning ensures that the study's goals, design, time-line, analyses, and budget do not diverge but, instead, are fully integrated and concordant with one another. Planning may be viewed as the reduction of uncertainty about what is feasible so that later surprises are prevented as much as possible. Good planning leads to a study that delivers high quality data that are relevant to the aims of the study and that are produced on time and within budget. Many early decisions are irreversible and influence the future course of a study and the use of available funds. Needless to say, these decisions need to be made with care.

Initially the goals of the study determine its design; however, during the planning phase, the goals may need to be adjusted because sample limitations dictate which questions can be answered. In addition, time and budget constraints set limits to the goals to be pursued. Thus, for a while, there is bound to be some flux in the goals and the design. In the end, however, one should have a plan in which each of the proposed goals is addressed in the design, time-line, analyses, and budget.

Often, studies founder because they were not planned adequately. Generally, insufficient planning leads to an overestimation of the ease of participant acquisition and the statistical power of a study and an underestimation of the time and budget necessary to execute a project. Funding agencies are seldom willing to increase the budget after a project is under way; consequently, insufficient planning may lead to a reduction in the scope of the project. Thus, in the end, practical matters, like money or participant availability, will dictate which goals can be reached in a particular study.

SPECIFIC PLANNING ISSUES

In this chapter we deal with specific issues of planning a study. We first consider issues related to the researcher's contacts with outside agencies, the community, and other researchers. These contacts may form the context of, or even the prerequisites, for a study. Other topics discussed in this chapter relate to the planning of the method of participant acquisition and data collection, the planning of a staff structure, and other issues concerning the logistics of data collection. These issues all have effects on the time-line of a study and on the budget necessary to accomplish one's goals. Planning a realistic time-line and budget are also discussed.

Cooperation From Agencies

Many studies *require* the cooperation of agencies like hospitals, schools, or courts to gain access to participants or to acquire data on an already existing sample. If agency cooperation is required, it is necessary not only to secure it in advance but also to clarify all *details* relative to obtaining access to records or to potential participants.

The fact that potential participant groups or records exist does not mean that a researcher has access to them (Hedrick, Bickman, & Rog, 1993). The first hurdle is to convince agency personnel that one's request is legitimate, that it serves an important purpose, and that it will not cost a large amount of agency time, energy, or money. Once there is some agreement in principle about access to records or to potential participants, the details need to be pinned down, preferably in written format. This process forces all parties to consider what is involved in the project and will help to prevent problems from surfacing when the work is about to begin (Ball & Brown, 1977).

Whereas agreement in principle is usually best discussed with the head of an agency, it is advisable to involve more agency personnel in the planning so that one will be less vulnerable if a change in leadership occurs. In addition, the details may need to be worked out with agency personnel directly involved with collecting and maintaining the agency's data. Decisions need to be made as to whether agency personnel, research staff, or a combination of both will search the records or make up the potential participant list. If it is determined that agency personnel will do the work, one needs to know how much it will cost, what a realistic time-line is, and what quality control procedures can be used. If the work will be done by research staff, it is important to find out when and where they will be allowed to do the work.

Contact With Agencies for Participant Acquisition. In studies relying on information from agencies for selecting and contacting the sample, the first priority is to ascertain how *current* the information is. For instance, one may be able to get a computer tape with names and addresses of students in certain grades; however, if the data were updated in September, the addresses may be of limited use in February in a district where people often move.

The possibility of errors in the data obtained from agencies needs to be taken into account. It is, therefore, always necessary to verify the accuracy of agency data, especially if they concern criteria for inclusion in the study. For example, some persons designated as males in a data file may turn out to be females, or some presumed 6-year-olds may actually be 5- or 7-year-olds. It is wise to request, in addition to basic information like names and addresses, other data like birth dates, aliases, parents' names, and Social Security numbers. This information will help to verify the identity of participants, to aid in locating participants if they have moved, and to facilitate later matching with other data sets.

Cooperation from an agency does not necessarily lead to cooperation from its clients because "clients" may have been forced to have contact with these agencies by the threat of legal action. An example would be participants in a court-mandated alcohol recovery program. Even if persons have willingly associated with an agency, as in the case of a voluntary admission to a psychiatric hospital, they may not want to be reminded of that particular episode in their lives. Potential participants from such agencies may be distrustful and refuse to participate just because of the connection of the investigator with the agency. Thus the potential of participant bias because of the connection of the researcher with the agency needs to be explored ahead of time.

Another example is that the approval of and cooperation with a study by school district administrators does not necessarily lead to the participation of teachers, who may feel put upon (Maruyama & Deno, 1992).

Data Collection From Agencies. Agency records may also be used to obtain new information pertaining to participants in a study or to validate interview data. The sources may be courts, schools, or medical agencies. Information from such sources can be an important part of a study, and procedures to obtain access to the data contained in such files needs to be planned carefully before the study begins. Questions that need to be addressed are: Are the records computerized and easily available or are they paper files that have been placed in storage? How complete and current is the information? How far back do the records go, and how long is current information kept? Are all records in the same format?

Agencies keep records for a variety of purposes, such as medical history, fiscal, legal, or year-end reporting. Their reason for keeping records may not require them to have their records in a particular order, to keep records beyond a certain period, or to be careful about the completeness and correctness of the information. Also, agencies may have changed the format of their records. Therefore, one may find that records are erased after a year, that there is no discernible system for identifying persons except by reading all records, that system-specific ID numbers are re-used and not unique, that the same participant may be found under different names, or that the way information is recorded changes over time.

One also has to be prepared to find potential bias in record keeping. An example may be achievement test results from schools. Weak students may stay away on the day of testing and schools may not mind this as it inflates their average test scores. It is, therefore, crucial to have a close look at the records before a study starts and talk to the personnel involved in compiling the records because they can point out weaknesses in the data that may not be immediately obvious.

Access to agency records is often restricted, and agency staff may have to identify and retrieve the files from which the research staff then extract the needed information. In this case it is important to plan with the agency how the record search will be conducted. Knowing that "factual" information like date of birth or name is far from foolproof, it may be necessary to encourage agency staff to search for participants creatively, for example, by names and aliases *and* by date of birth, or by address *and* Social Security number. This may be more easily done if the researcher is willing to pay for the work. Even then, agency staff will generally have to do this work in addition to their ordinary duties and may not relish extra work.

Thus when cooperation from agencies is needed—and for many social science studies such cooperation is essential—it is necessary to have time to prepare an agency, to find out what is possible and what is not, and to develop a working relationship that will benefit both the agency and the researcher.

A word of caution is necessary about providing agencies with information on participants for the purpose of record retrieval. For instance, addresses provided to an agency like the police to identify participants in their records can be used by them to find participants who are on the wanted list. Although participants may have given researchers permission to access agency data, we doubt that they would have done this had they foreseen an adverse outcome. Ethical considerations should preclude the researcher from exposing participants to risks resulting from sharing information about them with others.

Cooperation From Communities

Important early decisions that may affect the success of a study are whether to inform the community at large about an upcoming study, whether to enlist the support of community leaders, whether to form a community advisory board that can act as a facilitator if problems arise, or whether to keep a low profile and involve only those people directly necessary to conduct the study. It may seem good practice to inform the community about an upcoming study and to invite input. Indeed, there is much merit in using focus groups of potential consumers of the research to sharpen research questions. However, by involving the community, there are also risks that need to be considered.

The pros and cons of seeking community support need to be weighed carefully because a wrong decision may fatally affect the study. Although there are no hard data to tell us what to do, common sense may guide us through at least part of the decision-making process. Questions to keep in mind are:

1. How intrusive is the research design? Does it require an intervention that affects the whole or a large part of the community or a particular population, as in the case of a design of random allocation to services, classrooms, or interventions? If this is the case, the community needs to be involved in order to determine, ahead of time, whether the study can, in fact, be implemented.

2. How hostile is the community or the population of interest to the topic of study or to the persons conducting the study? If a study does not involve community interventions, is fairly noncontroversial, and is not expected to encounter community resistance, the best strategy may be to keep a low profile and involve only those persons necessary for the execution of the study. This strategy decreases the chance of negative publicity from disaffected persons, whose disaffection may be unconnected with the goal or execution of the study, and who may harm or even jeopardize the study.

Potential participants may, however, feel strongly that the *topic* is too sensitive or threatening, or that the *group* they represent is used for research purposes but does not benefit from the study or may be harmed by it. If such feelings threaten the execution of a study, it is necessary to enlist the support of community or group leaders to endorse the study and explain the potential usefulness of the results.

There is a danger, however, that in involving the community, one *fails* to enlist the support one is seeking and, instead, organized opposition is created. This could be the case, for instance, when asking a teachers' union to endorse teacher participation in a study not immediately related to the working conditions of teachers. Or, in areas or times of strong racial tension, minority leaders may not be swayed to endorse a study that is not seen as addressing their agenda. One way of reducing the chance of engendering such opposition is to *include* topics in the study that are high on the agenda of the persons one wants to have on one's side.

Media Contact

Often the topic of a study may be of interest to the public, and it may be tempting to respond to requests for information from the media. To decrease the chance of negative or incorrect publicity, it may be prudent to stay out of the limelight until the study is finished. There is, however, another reason not to appear in the media prematurely. Although participants should be informed about the study's general goals and procedures, they should not be influenced by giving them the opportunity to learn about the hypotheses and results of the study from the media. Also, in longitudinal studies, publicizing initial results may influence the participation rate or the answers given in later interviews.

Coordination With Other Research Groups

As part of the planning process it is necessary to find out what research is already ongoing or being developed that may impinge on the potential participant group necessary for the planned study. This is particularly important in cities with a concentration of universities with strong research departments. In general, it is not a good idea to use participants who are already participating in another study because the questions posed in one study may influence the answers given in another study, and the timing of the interviews may influence participation rates. In some cases it may be possible to combine one's research with another study by designing a common protocol requiring a single interview session for each participant. This solution requires careful delineation of tasks and territory, which is best specified in writing. At other times, it may be necessary to divide the "turf" or make an agreement about a time schedule for "competing" studies. As a last resort, when the field seems too crowded, one may wish to select another locale in which to conduct the study.

Preparation of Consent Forms

Federal and state laws require investigators dealing with human subjects to obtain a signed statement of informed consent from each participant before the research begins. Research institutions have an office, called the Institutional Review Board (IRB), that is charged with protecting participants from undue research risks and with providing investigators with guidelines for writing consent forms in the required format and language (for a good introduction to ethically responsible research, see Sieber, 1992). IRBs have to approve the procedures that the participant will be subjected to and the consent forms. The approval procedure takes time, and the investigator needs to allow enough time between the formulation of the final research protocol and the consent forms and the start of the study to ensure that IRB approval has been obtained.

Method of Participant Acquisition

What participant selection criteria are necessary to address the questions contained in the goals of a study? The goal of a study may be to describe the prevalence of criminal victimization in the population, compliance with a medical regimen among a specific group of organ transplant patients, or the relationship between parent involvement in homework and children's school success. The first example may require an extensive multistage sampling procedure to select households in which, for instance, the sample is stratified by census tracts with certain characteristics and addresses are randomly selected within each selected census tract. Depending on the study, certain persons may be selected for an interview, like males over age 18 or heads of households. These persons may be interviewed immediately or just listed and interviewed at a later point in time. This is a fairly involved procedure and can be quite expensive, especially when target participants are not found in every household, as would be the case, for example, for a study of parents of 3-year-old girls. In the example involving specific transplant patients, it may be possible to obtain lists of patients from the relevant hospitals and to study the whole population, because it is relatively small. In the third case, one could do a household sampling procedure to locate school-age children, or one could select school populations, knowing that certain students may be missed.

One other method of participant acquisition should be mentioned. For very difficult to acquire samples, researchers sometimes place advertisements in the local media or on billboards, or acquire the sample by word of mouth. An example of a difficult to acquire sample would be adult stutterers; they may not come to the attention of a particular professional group, and they may not have an organization dedicated to their problems. It may not be possible to say anything about the representativeness of such a sample, but it may be the only way to acquire enough participants who fulfill the conditions for inclusion in the study.

Apart from the issue of representativeness, there are issues of feasibility and cost. Clearly, for relatively rare research subjects, like severely mentally handicapped adults, one would want to start out with an identified sample rather than searching through many households to find them. Another reason for starting out with an identified sample would be that satisfaction of criteria for inclusion in the study could not be discovered by asking a few simple questions at the door, as would be the case, for instance, with some physical or psychiatric conditions. Starting out with an identified sample is, obviously, less expensive and time-consuming than having to undertake household sampling and enumeration procedures.

The ideal way of obtaining a representative sample is to give every potentially eligible person a known, nonzero chance of being selected for participation in the study (Henry, 1990). In practice, however, there are many barriers to accomplishing this ideal. Most of these barriers concern the time and money it would take to achieve a complete and accurate enumeration of the population of concern. Sometimes compromises are made consciously, as in the case where school-age children are selected from public schools but not from institutions, thereby missing a particular segment of children; at other times the sampling frame or list from which to select participants has shortcomings of which the researcher may not be fully aware. We come back to these problems in Chapter 5.

There are many excellent technical books and papers on sample selection, and the reader is referred to those for more details (Groves, 1989; Henry, 1990; Kalton, 1983; Kasprzyk, Duncan, Kalton, & Singh, 1989; Kish, 1965; Rossi, Wright, & Anderson, 1983; Sudman & Kalton, 1986). The decision of how to acquire one's sample is one of the earliest decisions that should be made. It will influence the design and time-line of the study as well as the conclusions that can be drawn.

Sample Size

How many participants does one need to study in order to address the goals that one has set? The answer to this question will, of course, affect the design and the budget, and it needs to be settled fairly early in the development of a project. The size of the sample is usually influenced by statistical considerations. One such consideration is the size of the standard error, which indicates the precision of an estimate derived from a study (Henry, 1990). Another is the need for power to detect statistically significant effects. One needs to keep in mind that many times specific analyses will be based on subsamples only, as in the case where one wishes to compare the characteristics of truant boys versus truant girls in a general school sample. Methods to calculate power and sample size can be found in Cohen (1977), Kraemer and Thiemann (1987), or Lipsey (1990). Other considerations with regard to sample size are the cost of the study and the availability of potential participants.

Method of Data Collection

Given the kind of questions one wants to answer in a particular study, what is the most appropriate form of data collection? Should one use mail-in questionnaires, do telephone interviews, conduct in-person interviews, or do observation studies in the lab or in naturalistic settings? Many studies have been conducted to show the relative merits of different forms of data collection, particularly with regard to participation rates and cost (Frey, 1983; Groves & Kahn, 1979; Hochstim, 1967; Miller, 1991). Of course, the type of data collection directly influences the cost of a study, with the mail-in questionnaire being the least expensive, followed by the telephone interview, the in-person interview, and direct observations as the most expensive. In the past, in-person interviews had a far higher response rate than mail and telephone procedures, but that advantage has been somewhat eroded by a reduced willingness or availability of people to be interviewed in person and by better mail and telephone procedures. Nevertheless, for long and complicated interviews, for interviews on sensitive topics, or for studies in which personal contact is important for continued participation over a period of time, an in-person interview is preferred.

A factor to take into account when deciding on the method of data collection is the safety of interviewers conducting in-person interviews in certain areas of inner cities. However, in areas that are not very safe, other data collection options may not work very well. Telephone inter-

views may not be useful because a considerable portion of the participants may not have access to a telephone. In addition, some inner-city
people move often, and others do not have a fixed address. Consequently, these people are not very easily reached by mail. Thus it may
be necessary to address the safety issue by hiring interviewers who
know these areas well or by teaming up interviewers rather than switch-
ing to an assessment mode that will yield a low participation rate.

In-House Data Collection or
Contract With Survey Organization

A decision of considerable importance is whether data collection and
data entry will be done in-house or contracted out. Because this book is
written from the perspective of conducting one's own research, it may
seem superfluous to discuss the second option. Nevertheless, we want
to point out the advantages and disadvantages of both options to make
the researcher aware that there are situations in which it may be advisable to make use of a survey research agency.

A reason for contracting out data collection may be that specialized
expertise, for example, for household sampling, is not available within
the research team or that data collection will take place over the whole
country and researchers want to make use of an existing network of
interviewers affiliated with a survey organization. Alternatively, researchers may feel that they do not have the inclination or expertise to
manage a large data collection effort, preferring to contract it out to an
organization that specializes in this work. Also, it takes time, which the
researcher may not have, to set up a smooth-running field operation,
whereas survey organizations have the infrastructure already in place.

We have chosen not to contract out our data collection, in part
because it would have been more expensive. Mainly, however, we felt
that with an outside agency, no matter how experienced and reputable,
we would not have direct control over the quality and completeness of
the data and the well-being of our participants. Unless there is an
independent quality control mechanism, the researcher has to rely on
the contractor's word that the work is of high quality.

Another disadvantage of contracting out data collection may be that
it is more difficult for the researchers to form an opinion on the meaning
of the data because the researchers are not directly involved in the
day-to-day decisions that are made while data collection is in progress.
These decisions may concern the interpretation of questions that prove

to be ambiguous or whether to stop trying to persuade a reluctant person to participate.

Also, interviewers working for a particular study rather than a survey organization may take greater care to ensure that participants have a positive opinion of the study because they feel directly responsible for the success of the study. This is particularly important in the case of longitudinal studies.

The pros and cons of in-house versus contracted data collection should be carefully considered because this decision has important implications for both the time-line and the budget. Reading the following chapters may clarify what is involved in data collection and may help to determine whether to undertake in-house data collection or to contract it out.

Key Personnel and Other Staff Issues

Before one can start to think about personnel, it is necessary to have a clear picture of the flow of *tasks* that need to be completed during the course of the study. Once one has an overview of the tasks, the next step is to combine the different tasks into staff positions and to organize the positions into some hierarchy for supervision and accountability.

Some tasks may be ongoing, such as the work of a secretary or a data analyst, whereas others may be cyclical, such as interviewing and the supervision of interviewers. A decision needs to be made whether a number of cyclical tasks can be combined into a year-round position or whether it is better to hire temporary staff. If cyclical tasks are combined, not all tasks in such a job cycle may have the same prestige, and prospective candidates for cyclical jobs need to be informed that their responsibilities will vary and that they may have to develop new job skills for off-season responsibilities. We return to this issue in Chapter 3.

A search for staff with practical managerial skills often conflicts with the need for individuals with research-oriented backgrounds. A case in point is the hiring of a project coordinator. This person is crucially important because the principal investigator looks to him or her to conduct the daily management of the project. A project coordinator should have a thorough, substantive background in the topic under study; be familiar with data collection; be able to hire, train, supervise, and manage staff; know how to prepare assessments; and be able to supervise computer programming, analyze data, and write reports. Finding such a person is like looking for a needle in a haystack.

Our solution has been to hire a number of supervisory people with complementary skills who function as a team. Each team member has his or her specialty and contributes to the development and documentation of procedures for conducting the study. The disadvantage of the team solution is that the principal investigator may not be able to concentrate entirely on data analysis and writing about the results but must also do some managing and coordinating.

Although it is possible, and sometimes desirable, to make changes in the personnel structure once it has been set up, such changes are often disruptive and time-consuming. It is, therefore, important to design a workable personnel structure ahead of time that distributes the tasks reasonably and comprehensively.

Where to Interview Participants

A number of considerations influence the decision about where to interview participants. The choices of location are generally interview rooms or lab space in one location, several interview rooms in areas where participants are to be found, or the participants' homes. Several factors need to be weighed to determine where to conduct the data collection. The first question to ask is whether the data collection *requires* a standardized setting because tests need to be administered or because cumbersome or calibrated equipment is involved.

Even if a standardized setting is not strictly necessary, there are many advantages to conducting interviews in offices rather than in participants' homes. The interviewer will not have to contend with interference from telephone calls, television, relatives, and other distractions, or problems like inadequate lighting and lack of writing space. Also, the interviewer will be more in control of the interview in the sense that the participant is the guest and may be less likely to engage in inappropriate behaviors, like drinking alcohol. In addition, the interviewer will not have to go to potentially dangerous neighborhoods.

Against these advantages of office interviews, there is one large disadvantage: many people do not mind participating in a study but they will not travel to an office to do the interview. Often, this is not a question of willingness but perhaps a lack of time or a baby-sitter, forgetfulness, fear of an unfamiliar place, or lack of money to pay for transportation. Although researchers can address some of these handicaps by offering larger sums of money, taxi vouchers, or baby-sitting services, interviews in the participants' homes usually yield a higher participation rate and a lower rate of broken appointments. An intermediate solution is to rent interview rooms close to where participants live (in schools, church buildings, or libraries).

If the decision is to use interview rooms, the number of rooms that may need to be rented to accommodate all interviewers may be quite large for some studies. At one stage in the Pittsburgh Youth Study we employed nearly 60 interviewers; it would have been extremely expensive to rent enough rooms to ensure that interviewers always had a room available when they needed to conduct an interview. This system would also have required a staff member to keep track of the room scheduling. Another consideration is whether the required number of interview rooms are available to be rented. The number of rooms that can be obtained or that one can afford to rent determines the number of interviewers who can be hired and, consequently, the speed with which an assessment phase can be concluded. In Chapter 4 we suggest ways in which the disadvantages of home interviews can be minimized.

Project Office Location and Layout

The location of the project office ideally should be determined by the decision about where the interviews will be conducted. If interviews will be conducted in interview rooms, the operation should ideally be located as close as possible to where the participants live. Even if the interviews are done in the field, it is best for the project office not to be too far away from "where the action is." Interviewers may need to come to the office to pick up more materials or to discuss difficult situations. Participants who have difficulty cashing their payment checks or who cannot wait until a check is mailed may want to pick up their money in the office. A project office that is close to where the participants live makes it easier for the investigators to stay more involved in the day-to-day management of the study by occasionally accompanying interviewers in the field or by interacting with participants who come to the office. If the office is farther away, or even in another city, it will take more planning, time, and effort for researchers to stay involved with interviewers and participants.

If interview rooms in the project office are utilized, it is important to have a *separate* section for the interview rooms so that other staff are not disrupted by the bustle of interviewing or by unknown persons wandering around. The separate interviewing section should have a waiting room. This is particularly important if there is a high volume of interviews or if the participants are children who need to be accompanied by an adult. Participants may bring their whole families; thus one should have the capability to make the participant's entourage comfortable and, if necessary, to baby-sit, feed, and entertain persons not strictly involved in the study (Marin & Marin, 1991).

Planning of the Interview Format

Another decision that needs to be made early is how the data are to be collected. Will traditional paper and pencil booklets, machine-readable forms, or laptop computers be used? We touch on the pros and cons of the various methods in Chapter 7. It suffices now to say that this decision has an effect on data entry staff, programming time, equipment, training of interviewers, and storage of interview materials.

Pretesting of Instruments and Procedures

One of the principal steps in the preparation of a study is conducting a pilot study in which participant selection and acquisition, interview schedules, and data collection are tried out. This is particularly important if any of the procedures are unfamiliar to the investigators or if the level of cooperation from potential participants or agencies is in doubt. When pilot testing is decided upon, enough time should be allowed to implement changes after the testing has taken place. Pilot testing may seem like an irritating holdup in the rush to acquire substantive knowledge. However, it is important to know beforehand whether the study one contemplates will, in all probability, be able to deliver the information one is seeking, and to do so within a certain budget and time-line. Furthermore, any proposal for external funding is greatly strengthened by prior pilot testing.

Planning for Data Entry and Data Management

Regardless of the mode of data collection, planning for how the data will be managed and reduced is essential if one does not want to end up with a large and costly mountain of undigested materials. What needs to be considered first is how incoming raw data will be tracked and stored. Adequate provisions need to be made for these requirements in the budget.

Next, one needs to consider the optimal time for data processing. Will data be coded, checked, and entered while data collection is still in progress, or will this be done after a data collection phase has been completed? If data processing is planned to occur after the field effort has been completed, there can be a more gradual build-up and training of staff, which may put less strain on the whole organization. The disadvantage is that it may take longer for the data to be available for analyses. More important, it does not allow one to catch data collection errors in time to rectify them.

Conventions for data reduction and data storage, and the creation and documentation of constructs, also require considerable planning and allocation of staff time. This is particularly important in studies where more than one person will be involved in the analysis of the data. Etiquette concerning the sharing of data with researchers outside the immediate study group is best organized beforehand and not after disappointments or problems have arisen (Sieber, 1991). Even within a research group it is good practice to decide, ahead of time, who is going to write on which topic.

TIME-LINES

Researchers need to have a clear idea how long it will take to produce results; otherwise, unrealistic expectations may be fostered that, inevitably, lead to disappointments. Unfortunately, many research proposals are formulated in such a way that there is too little time allotted for the different components of the research to be fully completed.

A common error is not to allow enough start-up time. Unless a project can be undertaken with existing staff, it will take from four weeks to six months to hire staff. Also, some staff members (like supervisors) may have to be hired and trained before the remainder of the personnel (like interviewers) can be recruited. The design, pilot testing, and printing of assessment instruments are other examples of tasks that may take several months from start to finish.

When studies depend on access to participants through agencies, like child welfare agencies, law enforcement agencies, or clinics, it will take time to develop a working relationship. Also, it may not be possible to recruit participants all at once. Instead, the recruitment may have to be spread out over a long period of time, depending on the case load of the agency. It is a common error to overestimate the ease of access to participants or the number of participants available. In order to obtain a high participation rate, it is necessary to have enough time to find elusive participants and to give reluctant participants time to change their minds.

Another pitfall is to underestimate the time that is necessary to process data to the point at which they are ready for analyses. Data entry and data cleaning (i.e., resolving inevitable errors by respondents, interviewers, and data entry staff) are necessary steps before data can be used. In addition, reducing raw variables to usable constructs is time-consuming. Enough time should be planned after data collection for data cleaning, making constructs, conducting analyses, and writing reports.

During the preparation for a study, very little attention is usually given to the time and human resources it takes to *document* all phases of the study. Adequate documentation becomes especially essential when large data sets will eventually become part of the public domain for use by people other than the original investigators. The time-line for final products from a study should take all these individual factors into account.

If most of the groundwork for the study, including pilot testing, building a working relationship with agencies, and careful planning of staffing, data collection, and data processing has been done in advance, the time-line for the actual study may be considerably shortened.

PLANNING A BUDGET AND
KEEPING IT UNDER CONTROL

When working out a proposed budget there is always the fear that the project will be too expensive to have a chance to be funded. However, this fear is usually coupled with a great optimism that, somehow, the work can be done if only one gets a grant. It is rare that this optimism is warranted; the more likely scenario is a reduction in scope of the project because there is not enough money to execute the design. This situation is often aggravated by administrative budget reductions in many federal grants.

In the actual execution of any study, there are always some budgetary surprises. However, too many unexpected expenses can cripple a project; therefore, it is prudent to *calculate, in advance, all costs in as much detail as possible.* Many of the individual budget items may seem minor and not worthy of the effort to calculate exactly; however, even small costs add up. For instance, the number of pages of each assessment instrument should be carefully estimated in order to accurately budget for the cost of duplicating interview materials. Likewise, mailing costs; trips to schools, agencies, or clinics; and the cost of project letterhead can be calculated instead of attempting global and often highly inaccurate estimates. Of course, multiyear studies need to provide for increases in costs over time.

Apart from making careful calculations, it is advisable to *eliminate as many uncertain costs* as possible. For instance, it may be possible to pay interviewers per completed interview rather than by the hour. In this way, not only is the exact cost of data collection known, but it also becomes unnecessary to keep track of interviewers' hours or check on the accuracy of their claims. The fee per completed interview can take into account the average number of miles it will take to obtain an interview, thereby avoiding paperwork for travel reimbursement requests.

Equipment repair is another instance of an uncertain cost. There may be no equipment breakdowns in a year or there may be a large number, taxing the budget. It may be advisable to have a repair contract after the warranty has lapsed, depending on how expensive the contract is compared to the cost of repair or replacement of equipment.

Even with the best planning there will be circumstances, like unexpected budget cuts, changes in procedures imposed by agencies, or higher duplicating costs, that force one to make adjustments in the budget in midstream. However, whatever can be foreseen should be dealt with ahead of time. Such planning leaves one with energy to deal with the truly unexpected crises.

Various books about proposal writing contain chapters about how to plan budgets. A reader wanting to consult a book for the purpose of making a budget might find Miller's *Handbook of Research Design and Social Measurement* (1991) and his references to other sources useful.

The careful planning of a budget is only the first step. One should also plan how to *keep* the budget under control while the study is in progress. A relatively spartan attitude toward spending may help. It may be possible for several staff members to share phone lines, printers, or other equipment that is not in constant use. Scrap paper can be used for environment-friendly note pads. Offices do not need to be luxuriously furnished, and some of them can be shared by people who are employed part-time. The aim is to turn as much as possible of one's budget into the business of high quality research rather than into unimportant trappings. Students may be able to take over some of the work of more highly paid employees, and sometimes it is possible to attract volunteers. It is best to plan to be frugal right from the beginning, because any scaling down afterward may be perceived as threatening by the staff.

Even with judicious spending, careful monitoring is necessary to ensure that the project stays within the total budget. Certain funding agencies require rebudgeting requests if the budget for a particular category is going to be exceeded. Such contingencies require even closer budget monitoring. In a university setting it may not always be possible to know, at any moment, how much of the study budget has been spent. Various departments, like Personnel and Purchasing, may process claims against the budget at different times, and a financial overview may be hard to obtain. Several solutions for this situation are possible and can be worked out in advance.

First one can request budget updates from the host institution on a regular basis. However, the accounting may be several months behind the actual expenditures and, therefore, may not help much in planning future expenses. If one's institution does not provide very satisfactory fiscal feedback, it does not hurt to request better service or to make suggestions for improvement. Even large institutions can make changes if the demand for these changes is extensive or if they will result in savings to the institution.

Second, one can plan to do one's own bookkeeping and hope that the figures will be close to those generated by the institution. However, this is often time-consuming and frustrating because purchasing prices may change or automatic salary raises may go into effect without the researcher's knowledge.

A third solution may be to decide to track only those expenses that are most in danger of being overrun, such as expenses that are not fixed, and rely on periodic institutional reports for the other expenses.

It is fair to say that, for most researchers, keeping track of one's spending is not the most popular activity. However, it is necessary to estimate the effect of a cost overrun in one area on the ability to execute the project as planned. If, for instance, the training of interviewers or the coding of materials takes four times as long as expected, one needs to consider what other expense can be omitted, as not absolutely essential, to pay for the unexpected expense. Alternatively, one can try to streamline the costly procedure. It is better to make conscious decisions rather than let matters take their course, only to find that some essential things cannot be done because money has run out. Thus keeping track of the budget needs to be incorporated as one of the tasks that will take time and money to accomplish.

CONCLUSION

It should be clear from this chapter that we consider careful planning a necessity in successful research and the management of financial resources. There is, of course far more to be said about planning than is contained in this chapter. Readers are referred to Hedrick et al. (1993) for more extensive coverage.

It may appear that the need to make so many decisions about how to conduct a study ahead of time may make the actual study a rigid, lifeless affair that, once started, runs a predetermined course. This is far from the case. One learns as one goes along and sees opportunities to improve organization, to distribute work differently, and to upgrade certain routines.

There needs to be a certain amount of structure in place right from the beginning, however, so that no fatal errors and not too many costly mistakes are made. The basic structure needs to be mostly correct from the start; from there on, one can go on "beautifying" the study at a more leisurely pace. In our own research operation we have, twice a year, a day of brainstorming with the whole staff about ways we can improve, and we have no trouble, after several years, in coming up with new suggestions.

3

Hiring

For investigators with little or no experience in conducting a research operation, hiring a competent and well-functioning staff can be an overwhelming and sometimes frustrating task. Decisions need to be made about what qualifications to look for in potential candidates, when positions should be filled, and for how long staff should be hired. Investigators have to become familiar with hiring policies, personnel rules, and equal opportunity guidelines. Finally, strategies have to be worked out to select the best-qualified individuals from the pool of available candidates.

This chapter deals with issues related to the development of an overall staffing plan, including hiring a research team with complementary as well as overlapping skills. We touch on the investigator's interactions with personnel departments and give suggestions on how to make them allies in the hiring process. We do not discuss hiring for all possible research positions but, rather, focus on hiring for the largest group of positions, the field data collectors. We also briefly address the hiring of coding and data entry personnel.

GENERAL ISSUES RELATED TO HIRING

After researchers have secured funding to conduct a study, one of the first tasks is to review and operationalize the staffing plan that was part of the research proposal. Changes in the design that were mandated by the review process or a reduction in funding may require that job tasks be redistributed to cover the work that needs to be accomplished in the final format of the study. New positions may have to be formulated, or, more likely, planned positions may have to be reduced.

Building a Personnel Structure

Especially in large studies, researchers have to consider a personnel *structure* in their hiring plan. Three distinct parts of the research effort need to be considered. First, the study needs data collectors, such as interviewers and interviewer supervisors; second, the study needs individuals who will be responsible for data entry, data cleaning, and documentation and who will prepare the data for analysis; and third, the study needs persons who will be responsible for the formal analyses and dissemination of the results. Depending on the size of the study, three separate teams for these different tasks may be formed. Researchers have to determine whether it is necessary to hire a study coordinator who can oversee all parts of the program or whether they want to recruit separate coordinators for data collection, data management, and data analysis.

The workload for each member of the research team needs to be clearly specified. Decisions have to be made about how many interviewers can be taken care of by one supervisor and how many research assistants a data manager is able to handle so that other tasks not directly related to supervision also can be accomplished. The workload of existing staff members needs to be reassessed as well. As a result of the start of the new project, secretarial staff may experience an increased number of telephone calls and may have to handle many more administrative tasks like processing time sheets or other personnel matters. Additional support in this area may have to be considered.

Researchers may also need to consider the possibility of promoting existing staff or students to new positions. Some of these individuals may have been involved in the planning of the study and may have helped to prepare the research proposal. Naturally, the investigator would like to retain people who are already knowledgeable about the upcoming study and are invested in its success. However, it is necessary to issue a word of caution against promising jobs too rashly. Initially, the greatest need is for people who are good at and willing to do the work involved in *conducting* a study. A graduate student who helped with literature searches or who pilot-tested an instrument in preparation for the proposal may not necessarily be the ideal person to fulfill the job requirements for supervising a data collection staff or managing data processing. Building an efficient research team may be severely handicapped if a new study is used to provide people with jobs regardless of whether they are the best suited to fill the positions.

Overlapping Skills. The individuals who are hired should have complementary skills so that all the tasks necessary for conducting the study are covered. It is, however, also important to build a team of individuals with partly overlapping skills so that any procedure that is crucial to the day-to-day operations of the project can be executed by more than one person. When other staff members are able to temporarily or permanently take over the tasks of an absent employee, the operation will not become paralyzed and hasty decisions about possible replacements can be avoided.

Interaction With the Personnel Department

In most cases the researcher is not the official employer of the research staff. The official employer may be a large entity like a university, a hospital, or a research organization. In that case the hiring process is regulated by a personnel department with a set of guidelines and rules. Personnel departments can be of tremendous help in searching for, interviewing, and choosing the most qualified candidates for the research team. However, personnel departments also can be a constraint when job descriptions need to fit preexisting employment categories, and starting salaries and pay increases are not controlled by the researcher.

When working with a personnel department to hire a number of staff members, it is useful to request that *one* personnel representative be assigned to the project to handle all issues related to hiring the research staff. This greatly simplifies interactions with the personnel department and avoids the possible confusion about who is working on what when more than one personnel official is involved with the project.

As the first step in the hiring process, the researcher should meet with the personnel official to explain the study but also to obtain information about employment regulations and the different steps involved in the hiring process. At such a meeting it is useful to discuss which responsibilities in the hiring process will be dealt with by the researcher and which tasks will rest with the personnel department. For instance, it is important to establish who handles job inquiries, who screens the resumes and calls references, and who covers certain topics in the job interview. Usually, the personnel official handles such issues as salary offers and the discussion about benefits, whereas the researcher is responsible for explaining job requirements.

There is another reason it is useful to talk with a personnel representative ahead of time. Researchers should be aware of questions that cannot be asked when interviewing prospective employees and should know the criteria that cannot be considered in selecting candidates. Personnel departments usually have guidelines that specify the kinds of questions that are inappropriate or illegal in a job interview, like inquiring about age, marital status, and having children. One should also be well informed about equal employment opportunity legislation before starting the hiring process.

If the researcher plans to use a set of standardized questions or rating scales to rank candidates, the personnel representative may need to review these documents to make sure they meet standards of fair hiring. It is also necessary to establish procedures to document hiring decisions and the length of time this documentation needs to be preserved. Sometimes, months or years after staff have been recruited, the personnel department may ask for detailed information on why certain candidates were not selected for a position.

Especially in recruiting for a new position, the personnel representative should have a clear understanding of the task requirements of the job and which qualifications are weighted more heavily than others. In selecting interviewers, for instance, tangible qualifications like education and previous job experience are sometimes less important than personal qualifications like flexibility and a pleasant interpersonal style. If personnel representatives are not aware of these considerations, they may question why an individual who only completed high school was preferred over a candidate with a bachelor's degree and telemarketing experience. Thus a close working relationship between the personnel representative and the researcher will expedite the hiring process and prevent selection problems.

Although it is time-consuming, researchers are usually well served to look at all job applications and not have a personnel officer pre-select candidates who meet the job specifications. Only the investigators have the overall picture of the different tasks that are needed for the project. They may be willing to compromise on some qualifications or to restructure some positions when they find a promising candidate with a good mixture of skills and experience.

FIELD STAFF
CHARACTERISTICS AND QUALIFICATIONS

Hiring a field staff may be the most challenging task for the researcher. Whereas investigators may be familiar with hiring secretaries or individuals who work on data analyses, they may be less familiar with hiring a team of data collectors. The field staff usually consists of supervisors and interviewers. In large projects, additional clerical support may be added to answer telephone calls and handle such administrative tasks as interviewer and participant payment. The best strategy is to hire interviewer supervisors first so they can assist in the preparation of the hiring process and the actual hiring and training of interviewers.

Interviewer Supervisors

What are the qualifications of a good supervisor? Most professional survey organizations agree that interviewer supervisors should have *past experience* with field interviewing, preferably in a research setting with similar objectives as the study under consideration. Interviewer supervisors should be highly organized and have the interpersonal skills to motivate interviewers to maintain high standards for the collection of reliable and valid data.

The task of supervising a group of interviewers can be quite taxing and supervisors need to be able to *structure* their workload. Interviewers frequently will place demands on supervisors' time to discuss problems, as will researchers who are anxious about the status of the field effort and data managers with questions about interview materials. Supervisors are the main collectors and distributors of the research materials. They have to make sure that interview booklets and other necessary forms are completed and received in the office and then channeled to the right individuals for further processing. If supervisors fall behind in their tasks, the rest of the research operation stagnates as well. As a result, participants may not be paid on time, or interviews may not be completed because participants have not been located. Thus it is critical that interviewer supervisors are able to do their work in an organized and timely manner, prioritize their tasks, and know when to alert their superiors if they are falling behind on their tasks. In our study, one full-time supervisor can effectively supervise up to a maximum of 25 part-time interviewers.

Supervisors also have to be extremely vigilant. Because interviewers cannot be directly observed in the field, the quality of interviews and the amount of effort that interviewers are investing in their job can be monitored only indirectly. Thus, supervisors should be able to track the interviewers' work carefully, be alert to changes in the interviewers' performance, and be prepared to take action when necessary. How to supervise interviewers successfully is covered in Chapter 6.

The supervisor needs to be a good listener and praise success and, if necessary, redirect effort. Interviewers should be able to use their supervisor as a *resource* for solving problems. Because they work mostly by themselves and do not have daily contact with coworkers, it is important that during supervision interviewers be given the opportunity to vent occasional frustrations and boast about their remarkable successes. At the same time, the supervisor has to be able to focus the interviewers' energies and help them find solutions to problems that may occur in the field. When interviewers feel that the supervisor pays attention to what they have to say and feel supported in their effort, they will become invested in the study and go the extra mile that is necessary to make the research a success.

Interviewers

Hiring interviewers who conduct high quality standardized interviews is one of the most crucial and also one of the most difficult aspects of a study. How well interviewers are able to retain participants in the project and how well they collect accurate and complete data will determine the quality of the research and its ultimate value. Researchers will have to decide whether they want to hire interviewers who have other jobs, whether it is necessary to hire interviewers with specific educational backgrounds, and whether it is advantageous or possible to match interviewer and participant according to race and/or gender. We will discuss each of these issues below.

How Many Interviewers? When starting the process of hiring interviewers, a decision needs to be made about the number of interviewers required to complete data collection on time. It may be tempting to overestimate the number of interviewers needed in case many drop out of the study or some turn out to be low producers. The decision to increase the number of interviewers needs to be considered carefully because having a larger interviewer pool raises training costs, increases time spent on supervision, adds to the administrative burden of the project, and may possibly affect the quality of the data.

In estimating the number of interviewers needed for the study, it is important to calculate how many interviews each interviewer on average can conduct in a given time period. This figure very much depends on the availability of participants. Especially in metropolitan areas, where a considerable downward trend in the proportion of people who are at home during daytime hours has been observed, the time available to conduct interviews in the home may be quite limited because most interviews have to be done in the late afternoon and evening hours

(Swires-Hennessy & Drake, 1992). For household interviews involving families, not all days or parts of the year may be equally good for interviewing. According to Vigderhous (1981), the best day of the week is Saturday until 4:00 p.m., with Thursday and Friday being the least productive days. January, February, and April have been considered the best months to do interviews, and December has been considered the worst. Also, a certain percentage of broken appointments needs to be taken into account when calculating the number of interviews that each interviewer can complete in a particular period.

Full-Time Versus Part-Time Interviewers. Given the availability of respondents, the size of the sample, and the time-line of the study, it should be possible to estimate in advance a reasonable number of interviews that each data collector has to complete in a specified time period. This number should be taken into consideration when selecting candidates. It may seem a good idea to hire interviewers without any other work commitments on the premise that they can devote all their time to the study. However, in our experience, candidates with daytime employment but with sufficient time to work in the evenings and on weekends can be just as productive as candidates with no other employment. In addition, persons with no other job may be actively looking for more permanent work and may leave as soon as a job more suited to their needs becomes available. The point is to hire people who are available at the times that interviewing needs to be done and who, most likely, will continue with the project through the entire interview phase.

Seasonal Versus Year-Round Interviewers. In longitudinal studies with fairly regular assessments, it is important to consider whether it is desirable to retain interviewers between assessment waves. Some projects provide the interviewing staff with clerical duties like coding and data entry when no data are being collected. Although this strategy may prevent field staff from drifting away to more permanent employment, it can be costly because interviewers usually earn higher wages than clerical personnel. Also, it is not always easy to motivate interviewers to return to the field after they have enjoyed temporary office jobs. On the other hand, training may be so expensive (as in the case of studies using observation techniques or clinical interviews) that the data collection staff, once trained, is worth retaining during off-season periods. Another reason for maintaining interviewers is that researchers may want to pair interviewers and participants for the duration of the study in order to build rapport. Alternatively, however, researchers may require interviewers to be *blind* to information obtained in previous data collection waves, which entails either the careful juggling of interviewers or the hiring of new interviewers for each assessment wave.

General Characteristics. Do interviewers who are similar to the respondents in age, education, and social class obtain more valid interviews than those who are not? Although demographic similarities may have a positive effect on the relationship between the interviewer and the respondent, studies show that concordance of demographic characteristics does not necessarily lead to better reporting (Davies & Baker, 1987; Groves, 1989; Weiss, 1968).

Should interviewer and participant be matched according to ethnic background or gender? There is an abundance of literature on race-of-interviewer effect on respondents (for a review, the reader may consult Anderson, Silver, & Abramson, 1988). Significant effects that have been detected are mostly related to racial attitudes. When interviewed by African American interviewers, African American respondents generally express less positive feelings about Caucasians, and Caucasians as well as African American respondents offer more liberal opinions on questions related to racial issues. Concerning other questions not directly related to racial issues, no consistent differences between African American and Caucasian interviewers have been found.

Similarly, studies addressing the impact of the gender of the interviewer on questions related to sexual attitudes and other gender-sensitive domains have shown that both male and female respondents are more critical of gender inequalities when they are interviewed by female interviewers. For other kinds of questions, the results have been far less conclusive (Groves & Fultz, 1985; Kane & Macaulay, 1993).

Although interviewer gender may not be of great importance for the way participants answer questions, respondents generally react more favorably to female than to male interviewers in terms of overall performance, friendliness, and participation rates (Fowler & Mangione, 1990; Groves & Fultz, 1985). Higher participation rates have also been observed among older interviewers. This effect was independent of interviewing experience, which suggests that some quality related to age was responsible for the effect (Singer, Frankel, & Glassmann, 1983).

Thus, except for interviews that cover specific attitudinal topics, there is no reason to believe that female participants report more truthfully when interviewed by women as opposed to men; that college students, because of their closeness in age, are better suited for interviewing older adolescents; or that surveys concerned with family inter-action and child rearing are better served by hiring as interviewers women who have children. Hiring middle-aged female interviewers, however, may be important when soliciting initial cooperation from women or retired people, who may be reluctant to let a young male interviewer, whom they do not know, into their house. The gender and age of the interviewer are expected to be less of an issue for follow-up interviews when the participants are already familiar with the study.

Personal Characteristics and Qualifications. Field interviewers should be pleasant and streetwise people who have self-assurance in dealing with people. They should be open-minded and able to keep their opin-ions to themselves. Interviewers should be self-starters, able to work independently, and good at following instructions. Usually, the need for additional income is a good motivator to become a productive inter-viewer.

Minimum Qualifications. Most research organizations require inter-viewers to have at least a high school diploma with excellent reading and writing abilities. Occasionally, more advanced degrees will be necessary for interviewing that involves complicated data sampling procedures or a large number of open-ended questions that require special probing techniques or that rely to a great extent on interviewer judgment. Surveys covering very sensitive topics, like the effect of suicide on relatives, may want to employ clinical professionals rather than lay interviewers to minimize the possible risks resulting from the effect of being interviewed (Turnbull, McLeod, Callahan, & Kessler, 1988). However, in general, too much education may be somewhat of a liability in that it may increase the risk of the interviewer asking leading questions or over-interpreting responses. Researchers do not need mini-investigators as interviewers; they need data collectors who can adhere to the way they have been trained to ask questions and record answers.

In general, previous interviewing experience is considered desirable (Cleary, Mechanic, & Weiss, 1981; Singer et al., 1983). Seasoned data collectors usually have the confidence that they can do the job, are not as easily discouraged by reluctant respondents as newly trained inter-viewers, and may be better at creating a secure environment in which the interviewee feels confident answering sensitive questions. On the other hand, experienced interviewers may have developed ways of conducting interviews that differ from the standards of a particular study. These interviewers may be more difficult to train than novice interviewers because they may find it hard to unlearn their previous habits. Burnout may occur more frequently among interviewers who have been working on surveys for a long time. As a consequence, these interviewers may become much harder to motivate in pursuing reluctant or hard-to-find respondents than their less seasoned but not entirely novice counterparts.

HIRING PROCESS FOR INTERVIEWERS

Hiring a large number of interviewers can be a tedious and time-consuming process. To make it less so, we have deviated from traditional face-to-face interviews and have developed the following strategies for hiring a large number of interviewers in a short period of time. The first step in the hiring process is to advertise in local newspapers, weekly bulletins, and community circulars. The announcement should include *all details* that are crucial in making a decision about applying for the job. For instance, if the employment is part-time and temporary, has limited benefits, and requires weekend and evening hours, these facts should be specified in the advertisement.

Group Information Sessions

In the advertisement, individuals are invited to attend one of several group information sessions. These sessions should be held at prime interviewing times (e.g., in the late afternoon and early evening hours) to deter people who usually have other commitments during these time periods from attending. The group format makes it possible to simultaneously inform many potential candidates about the study and the conditions of the job, thereby eliminating the need to repeat the information to each interested person in a face-to-face interview.

In the first part of the group information session, a short overview of the research project is presented, the objectives of the study are explained, and all job requirements are spelled out in detail. Special attention is given to the fact that interviewers must be willing to do interviews wherever they need to be done. This may discourage some persons who are hesitant to travel to certain neighborhoods. Although the availability of a car may not be used as a criterion for employment, it should be stressed that without access to reliable transportation, the job cannot be done efficiently. It is also important to emphasize that interviewers should be available at the times that respondents prefer to be interviewed. The hours that are good to do interviews may not necessarily coincide with the times that some potential candidates have available for the job. To control the flow of the interviews and make the data collection effort timely and cost effective, we also tell those in attendance that we expect each interviewer to complete a minimum number of interviews in a specified time period. This requirement may exceed the time commitment that the candidates had in mind. Thus, all *potentially negative aspects of the job* are clearly spelled out so as to discourage applications from unsuitable candidates.

Next, a member of the research staff with previous interviewing experience provides information about the nature of the job from a personal point of view. This individual tells potential candidates what it was like to become an interviewer and what was needed to be successful. A representative of the personnel department is also present to answer technical questions concerning the conditions of employment.

Individuals who are still interested in the job after hearing the first part of the information session are invited to participate in the second part of the meeting, which involves completing personnel forms. Candidates are also asked to indicate on a provided calendar their present time commitments and to write a brief essay about their desire to become an interviewer or about unique qualifications they may have for this type of work. They are required to enclose their resume with these forms.

From the material obtained in the information session, applicants who do not have the appropriate qualifications or who have jobs that are too closely related or even conflicting with the interests of the study are eliminated from further consideration. In general, interviewers should not have any reason to encounter (or have encountered) the participants in their other professions. This level of anonymity prevents any conflict of interest on the part of the interviewer and also ensures that participants feel that they can answer questions freely.

Applicants whose current time commitments conflict with the hours that interviewers are expected to work are also omitted from the list of possible candidates. The way personnel forms are filled out in the group session may give an indication of how well candidates follow instructions on forms and how legibly they write, which is important when the means of data collection is to complete interview booklets. The personal essay allows for some assessment of the appropriateness of the applicants' motives and expectations about the work. Finally, individuals who arrived very late at the group sessions, behaved inappropriately, made hostile comments, or asked inappropriate or irrelevant questions can be elmiminated from the list of prospective candidates.

Personal Interview

The next step in the hiring process is to invite selected candidates to meet with a recruiter. In our study, usually two supervisors are involved in interviewing prospective candidates; both interview each candidate with a *well-prepared script of questions* to keep the evaluation process as consistent as possible. A large portion of the personal interview should be used to get an idea of the applicants' interpersonal skills and to evaluate the manner in which they communicate with the recruiter.

Trainability and flexibility are essential but difficult characteristics to evaluate. Interviewers should be able to absorb a great amount of instruction in a short period of time and later follow these instructions when conducting the interview. Because all candidates have attended the information session, we ask them in the personal interview what they remember about the study from the meeting in order to get some indication of how well they are able to retain information.

Although interviewers should conduct interviews in a standardized manner, they should also be able to find creative solutions to unforeseen problems. A way to test the candidates' flexibility is to give some examples of problems that may arise in the field and see if they can come up with creative solutions. For instance, the interviewer may ask the applicants what steps they would take to find a street that does not exist on any road map or what they would do when they make a household visit and discover that the participant does not live there any longer.

If the study deals with sensitive topics, it is important to ascertain how the applicant feels about asking the participant questions related to these issues. The investigator may not want to hire applicants who express some reluctance about dealing with potentially delicate questions or who expect that certain questions will be difficult to handle. By the same token, a missionary attitude to the topic that leads to over-involvement may not be conducive to obtaining an accurate response from a respondent either.

In the personal interview, we also make a point of going over the time calendar that each participant filled out during the group information session. Interviewers cannot be effective if they are not able to conduct interviews when participants are available. Some candidates may have thought only about their work commitments when filling out the calendar and may not have realized that they should have marked off additional time periods for recreational or religious activities. An overestimation of the time that the potential candidate has available coupled with an underestimation of the time it takes to do an interview are the most likely reasons for failure in a beginning interviewer.

Mock Interview

As part of the application process, applicants are required to conduct a mini mock interview with the recruiter. Before starting the mock interview, the candidate is given a few minutes to look over the interview, read the instructions, and ask questions. For the applicant, the mock interview shows the kind of instruments that are used in the study. Especially for individuals who have never been interviewers, it is helpful to be confronted with the complications of having to read questions and record responses. For the recruiter, the mock interview serves as a tool to assess the candidates' ability to give clear instructions, to make appropriate eye contact with the recruiter, to read questions exactly as stated, to follow skipping patterns, and to record the answers accurately. The mock interview is also a good way to evaluate the voice quality of the candidates. To be effective in the role of data collector and keep the attention of the respondent, interviewers should have variation in their reading, have a distinct pronunciation, and read loudly enough for the participant to hear the questions without effort (Oksenberg, Coleman, & Cannell, 1986).

Final Selection

Before the final selection takes place, references need to be checked. During the personal interview, the recruiter should review the references with the candidate to make sure that individuals who are listed as references can provide relevant and recent information on the candidates' qualifications and work skills. Contacting *personal* references should be avoided as much as possible. If a representative from the personnel department does the reference checking, this person should be briefed on obtaining information related to skills and qualifications that are relevant to the job of interviewing. A former or current employer providing a reference may not be able to comment directly on interviewing skills but may be able to say something about the candidate's ability to be a self-starter, to take initiative, and to find creative solutions in difficult situations.

We always select more interviewers than are necessary. Some candidates, who are between jobs, will keep searching for more permanent employment and may find another job by the time training begins. Others discover during training that they do not like the job, and still others successfully finish training but for some reason will be unsatisfactory interviewers. In our experience, about 35% to 50% of individuals who attend the group information session are invited to a personal interview, and about half of these are offered the job. Some candidates are eliminated or leave voluntarily during training; the percentage of these dropouts can be as high as 30%. Altogether, not more than 20% of the original group of individuals who attended the information sessions will be left when data collection gets under way. Similar percentages have been observed by survey organizations using more traditional face-to-face hiring techniques (Davis & Smith, 1992).

Rehiring Veteran Interviewers

In longitudinal studies with multiple assessment waves, researchers have to consider whether they want to rehire interviewers who have worked previously for the project. To work with interviewers who are familiar with the project is attractive. Their past work history is known, and it is convenient to have veteran interviewers available to help with training exercises and to accompany new interviewers on observation interviews.

In considering veteran interviewers for re-employment, it is important to realize that past productivity is not always a sure predictor of future performance. Veteran interviewers may burn out after a few assessment waves, or their personal circumstances may change in such a way that they are less available to work for the project and are not able to conduct the required number of interviews. It also has been demonstrated that the longer interviewers work for a study, the more they begin to take liberties with the way the interview should be administered (Fowler & Mangione, 1990). This variation can, of course, be reduced by retraining veteran interviewers at every assessment wave and by vigilant supervision. It should not be a foregone conclusion that veteran interviewers will be rehired. Their previous performance should be carefully assessed, and their availability to conduct interviews should be scrutinized before they are selected.

HIRING DATA PROCESSING STAFF

For coding, data entry, and data checking, research projects that are part of a university environment often hire college students to work part-time during the academic year. Coding may require the employment of graduate students or undergraduates with an academic interest related to the study, whereas most data entry and data checking jobs can be done by individuals with a high school diploma.

In the lives of many students, having a job is a necessary evil but not something that requires much thought or dedication. In addition, these young people may not have much job experience and may have to be taught elementary work habits like being conscientious and on time, not socializing extensively with coworkers during working hours, or not receiving a large number of personal phone calls. Productivity needs to be tracked constantly.

If many part-time students are employed by a project, keeping track of research assistants (RAs) can become an administrative hassle. Work hours for these RAs have to be arranged around their class schedules, schedules need to be arranged and rearranged, and computers need to be available for different people at different times. One solution is to designate Saturday as a mandatory work day so that all RAs can be present at the same time. This arrangement makes it easier to schedule a weekly meeting for announcements and the discussion of problems and procedures. RAs responsible for the coding of the interview schedule can get together with their supervisor to resolve coding issues that need the attention of the whole coding staff. Such a schedule also allows the use of computers for data entry that are not available during the regular work week because they are used by full-time regular staff members. To make the job more interesting, increase job satisfaction, and decrease attrition among RAs, it is a good investment to occasionally schedule training and information sessions that cover such topics as computer software, career planning, and discussions about the findings of the study. The Saturday hours are often attractive to students, and the offer of extra training and information may give the job an edge over other jobs available on campus.

After many years of hiring staff, it is still difficult to always correctly predict productivity and tenacity in candidates. Thus, even with good hiring strategies, there will always be individuals for whom employment in a research project does not work out. However, investigators can make the job a positive and rewarding experience for most of the research team by providing adequate training and a supportive environment that nurtures confidence in doing the job right. These last two issues are covered in Chapters 4 and 6.

CONCLUSION

Before starting the hiring process, researchers need to develop a staffing plan and consider a personnel structure that can cover the work that has to be accomplished. A good understanding of the hiring policies and the role and the level of involvement of the institution's personnel department greatly facilitates the process of hiring a research staff. Systematically following carefully prepared hiring steps helps researchers to select candidates with the right mixture of experience, qualifications, and characteristics to do their job successfully.

4

Training of Interviewers

The success of most studies depends to a great extent on the interviewers' ability to convince respondents to participate and to administer interviews in a standardized manner. The training of interviewers, therefore, should focus on optimizing interpersonal skills and teaching the correct interviewing techniques. When data collection starts, interviewers should be fully able to do their job as required and their first interviews should be *up to standard* and not be deficient because of lack of training. In other words, the initial time on the job should not be treated as a learning period in which skills are allowed to improve gradually; interviews done early in the assessment phase should be of the same high quality as interviews done later (Fowler & Mangione, 1990).

The focus of this chapter is on how to train data collectors who administer interviews in the homes of participants. We discuss how to plan and organize the training and deal with conditions of employment and legal and ethical issues related to the job of interviewer. We also consider issues such as how to train interviewers in gaining cooperation from participants, how to prepare for the interview, and how to use correct interviewing techniques.

Many issues and techniques that are covered in this chapter also apply to training of interviewers who work in other settings, like interviewers who administer interviews in offices or who collect information on the phone. The preparation for and the content of the training that we describe are not unique to large studies. If a study uses only 2 interviewers, they should be trained just as carefully as when 15 interviewers are needed.

PLANNING THE TRAINING

Many decisions need to be made when preparing a training course for interviewers. Who should conduct the training? How long should it last? What should be covered, and is it necessary to have a training manual?

For the training to be effective and to make sure that all training issues will be included, it is necessary to spend sufficient time planning every aspect of training ahead of time.

Who Conducts the Training?

The task of training interviewers usually rests on the shoulders of the interviewer supervisors but may include other members of the research team as well. For instance, the investigator may want to explain the goals of the study to the interviewers and stress the importance of collecting high quality data. Data managers can be helpful in teaching interviewers to obtain appropriate responses to questions that need a descriptive answer, which may not only benefit the interviewers but also greatly facilitate the coding, cleaning, and interpretation of these responses.

Planning Training Hours

Training dates should be established before the hiring process gets under way. This enables recruiters to review the training schedule with the applicants and to eliminate prospective candidates whose other obligations conflict with training hours. It may be helpful to schedule the training sessions during peak interview hours; this is an effective way of finding out whether interviewers are truly available during these times.

Duration of Training

How many training hours are required to prepare interviewers for their job? It is not necessarily true that the longer the interviewers are trained the better they perform in the field. Scheduling too much training time may be counterproductive, as has been illustrated by Fowler and Mangione (1990) in their study comparing the performance of interviewers assigned to different training classes that varied in length and content. Training that is too long and that devotes too much time to possible stumbling blocks may create uncertainty and insecurity in interviewers instead of raising their level of competence. On the other hand, the training should be long enough to enable interviewers to become completely familiar with all interview materials, to feel confident in dealing with participants, and to use the correct interviewing skills.

It is tempting to complete the training as quickly as possible so that interviewers can go into the field and data collection can get under way. Each training session, however, should last not longer than a few hours, and the training schedule should allow sufficient time for review and preparation. Interviewers need time *between* training sessions to absorb the materials that have been discussed in class, complete homework assignments, prepare for classroom tests, and look over sections of the training manual that will be covered in the next training session. The staff members responsible for the training also need time between training sessions to assess the progress of each trainee. They have to correct homework assignments and, if necessary, make adjustments to upcoming training sessions to more closely address the needs of the interviewers. Spacing the training sessions allows for the most efficient use of training time.

Our training of field interviewers generally consists of a total of 18 to 20 hours' training to master interviewing techniques, to learn how to fill out forms, and to become familiar with a 2½-hour interview. This does not include supervised practice that takes place after the classroom training has been completed. The training schedule usually starts with 6 hours of training on a Saturday and, in the following week, continues with 3-hour training sessions in the evening hours on alternate days. More complex surveys with complicated skipping patterns or inter-views that require interviewers to make judgments may need longer training hours. Some interview modes, such as telephone interviews, generally require less training. However, no matter what method of data collection is used, interviewers should be allowed to interview actual participants only when the instructor is completely satisfied that the interviewers can handle *all* aspects of the job. Some flexibility should be built into the training schedule to allow for additional training hours if they are necessary.

Training Veteran Interviewers

In longitudinal studies, some interviewers may continue to be em-ployed by the project for several data collection periods. Although the training of veteran interviewers for a new interview phase can be less extensive than the training of new interviewers, they should definitely receive training. The reason for this is that experienced interviewers tend to become more casual in the way they administer the interview (Groves, 1989). They are inclined to make more errors in reading the questions exactly as worded and begin to deviate from using the correct probing techniques (Fowler & Mangione, 1990). Therefore, the training of veteran interviewers should focus on reiterating the basic rules of standardized interviewing.

A distinction should be made between veteran interviewers who were employed in the study during previous assessment waves and experienced interviewers who previously worked for other research projects. For interviewers with previous data collection experience outside the project, some of the training may be familiar and somewhat repetitive. However, all organizations train their interviewers differently, and the interviewing standards of other projects may not be the same as the standards of the present study. Thus interviewers with previous experience should be trained with new interviewers, and their performance should be carefully monitored during training to make sure they do not continue old habits.

The Role of the Interviewer During Training

No matter how many hours are invested in the training of interviewers, the instructions are of little use if interviewers do not take the training seriously. Interviewers should be expected to read the manual, prepare the materials that will be covered in each training session, arrive on time for the training sessions, participate in classroom exercises and role playing, and finish all homework assignments. If the performance of trainees is below standard, they should not be promoted to the status of interviewer and should be discontinued from the study.

Without exception, attending all training sessions should be *mandatory*. Having to schedule additional training hours for people who have missed sessions is not only a major irritant but also time-consuming and expensive. An added inconvenience may be that additional training hours have to be scheduled after data collection has started. At that time the project's staff is occupied with lending support to interviewers already in the field and may have little time for teaching additional training classes. These are enough reasons to insist that interviewers attend all regularly scheduled training sessions.

The Role of the Instructor

Instructors should consider their task as laying the foundation for the success of the study. Effective instructors convey to the interviewers that their performance is important and that high quality interviews are the only interviews worth doing. The instructors should make sure that all interviewers are actively involved in the training and that all classroom exercises and homework assignments are completed. At the end of training, the instructors should evaluate the interviewers and determine whether they are ready to go into the field. During training, they should maintain documentation that allows for the elimination of interviewers whose performance was not satisfactory.

The Training Manual

Developing a training curriculum is best achieved by writing a *comprehensive* manual. Although the preparation of a training manual is time-consuming, it forces instructors to think ahead about issues that need to be covered during the actual training. The manual should contain *all* the information interviewers need to do their job. Ideally, the layout of the training manual should follow the same order as the topics covered during the training sessions. If interviewers are trained at different times or by different instructors, the manual ensures that everyone receives the same information and standardizes the way the study will be conducted. The manual also functions as a reference tool to be consulted after the training is completed; therefore, the manual should have a table of contents.

Planning of Individual Training Sessions

Training interviewers is expensive. Therefore, every minute of the training should be planned, and training schedules should be worked out before the training begins. The schedule needs to include a detailed list of all the topics that are covered in each training session, together with the amount of time devoted to each topic.

Besides general information about the study and instructions on how to administer the interview, good training covers such topics as the legal aspects of the study, conditions for employment, how to contact participants, and how to deal with refusals. All forms that are used in the interview, like contact sheets, consent forms, and payment request forms, should be discussed; interviewers should know which forms should be used when and how they should be filled out. An important part of the training should be the acquisition of interviewing techniques such as how to clarify questions and probe for additional answers. In the remainder of this chapter, we touch on a number of practical and technical training techniques that we believe are effective or helpful for interviewers, without trying to exhaust all possible training topics.

GENERAL TRAINING ISSUES

Conditions of Employment

Although the conditions of employment have been discussed with the interviewers during the hiring process, these issues should be addressed again during training. Interviewers usually are attracted to the job because they enjoy the flexibility and relative independence that is inherent in this type of work. Some interviewers, however, may have trouble with the lack of day-to-day structure of the job and find it difficult to stay motivated. A written policy statement that outlines the job requirements is a helpful document to ensure that every interviewer understands the obligations of employment. Such a policy statement may include specific details concerning attendance at regular office meetings with supervisors, the completion of a minimum number of interviews in a specified time period, and not having more than a certain percentage of refusals and errors. When interviewers handle expensive equipment like computers and testing devices, or carry participant payment moneys, the researchers should make sure that the interviewers understand the consequences of failure to return office property when employment is terminated.

When dealing with employment issues, the remuneration of interviewers should be addressed in detail. Interviewers who are paid by the hour should be informed how the time they spent working on an interview will be recorded. For instance, they should know whether travel time to the participant's house and time spent trying to contact participants by phone will be included in their hourly pay. When interviewers are paid by the interview, they should have a clear understanding of when an interview is considered to be complete and is released for payment. Interviewers should sign a policy statement containing conditions of employment, and a copy should be retained by them for reference. This policy statement should be legally binding, and failure to adhere to the conditions of employment may be grounds for dismissal.

Legal Obligations and Ethical Issues

Interviewers need to be made aware that their relationship with participants entails certain legal responsibilities and limitations. For instance, they need to know that their contact with participants is restricted to the task for which they were hired, data collection. The importance of adhering to these rules cannot be overemphasized because one infraction of the rule can jeopardize the continuation of the entire study.

It cannot be stressed enough during training that no interview can be done before all prescribed procedures for obtaining informed consent are completed. These procedures include explaining the content of the consent form to participants, giving participants ample time to read the consent form or reading the consent form to them, asking participants if they have any questions, and having the consent forms signed.

For adult participants the consent forms should be written in a language that can be easily understood by sixth grade students. For younger children who give consent, the language needs to be adjusted to a level that they can comprehend. The consent form needs to include a description of all the steps involved in and the possible risks attached to participating and how much the participant will be paid. In addition, participants should be assured that all information that the interviewer obtains is confidential, with the possible exception of a few circumscribed cases like child abuse or life-threatening situations.

The confidentiality of all information obtained from participants should be carefully adhered to. Telling funny or horror stories about participants just for amusement, even if names are omitted, should not be permitted. In addition, it is good practice to refer to the persons who take part in a study as "participants" and not "subjects" to avoid dehumanizing them in any way. It should also be emphasized during training that interviewers keep completed interview materials in a safe place. In their homes, they should be locked away so that other members of the household cannot accidentally read the materials. Only interview materials necessary for the work at hand should be in a car and, even then, should not be visible to passersby.

Interviewers need clear guidelines on how to act in cases of actual or suspected child abuse or potentially life-threatening situations. There are wide-ranging interpretations of what constitutes child abuse. The laws governing the reporting of child abuse and neglect vary in different states, and institutions have different ways of handling suspected cases of abuse. It is, therefore, important that investigators have a clear understanding of the specific rules and conditions that apply at their study site. Procedures for interviewers may be developed in consultation with the legal department of the sponsoring institution.

Only in very rare cases will interviewers witness an incident that warrants *immediate* intervention to protect the life or health of another individual, necessitating discontinuation of the interview and immediate reporting of the incident to the police or child protective services. In most situations, interviewers either may witness *possible* child abuse that is not immediately life threatening or may suspect child abuse because, for instance, a child shows his or her bruises or tells about severe beatings. In these instances, interviewers should not act on their own. They should document what they have seen and heard and get in touch with their supervisor as soon as possible. The supervisor should determine what the next step will be. The documentation should be extensive and timely because it may not be so easy without written notes to remember the exact details of an event when the interviewer is questioned about it later. Large institutions like hospitals may have incident forms that cover the relevant areas to which interviewers need to respond when observing child abuse.

Personal Safety

Although it is not possible to guarantee the personal safety of the interviewers in the field, interviewers should be instructed in how to minimize the risk of being victimized on the job. Most police departments have officers who are trained to talk about safety issues to groups in the community. Safety experts should be briefed in advance about the specific working conditions of interviewers to enable them to make their talk relevant to people doing fieldwork.

Interviewers should be trained to reduce their chances of being victimized by looking and walking purposefully and by knowing what to do when their car breaks down. If interviewers become concerned about their personal safety inside the residence of a participant, they should be trained that they always have the option to discontinue the interview. There are ways to interrupt an interview without being discourteous. As a precautionary measure interviewers may try to position themselves in such a way that they can exit the premises without their path to the door being blocked. In summary, interviewers should be trained to always use common sense while they are in the field and not to expose themselves unnecessarily to potentially dangerous situations.

Getting to Know the Core Office Staff

Interviewers should become familiar with the general personnel structure of the office. In multisite studies it may not be possible for interviewers to meet all the members of the research team during training, but it is important that they know who the key people in the operation are. A list of staff members, with their primary functions and telephone numbers, should be provided to the interviewers. If, in an emergency, they cannot reach their supervisor, they can consult this list and contact the appropriate person.

When the study office is in the same location as the interview site, members of the office staff should always make the interviewers feel welcome and appreciated when they come to the office and include them in office social events. Interviewers are the backbone of most research studies but tend to be overlooked because they spend most of their time in the field, and their interaction with staff members other than their supervisors may be sporadic. When interviewers feel that they are an integral part of the research team and that their work is important and valued, they do a better job.

Getting to Know Other Interviewers

Because interviewers work mostly independently, they rarely have the opportunity to meet their fellow interviewers. It is important that interviewers get to know their colleagues, feel like part of a group, and support each other when necessary. In the first training session, such interaction can be facilitated by having pairs of interviewers interview each other with some innocent questions like "What would people be surprised to find in your refrigerator?" or "What is your favorite building in town and why?" The task is completed by asking each interviewer to report on his or her teammate to the group. The exercise breaks the ice among the interviewers and, at the same time, gives them a sampling of what it is like to interview and be interviewed. Also, interviewers will get to know each other by working together on homework assignments or practicing interview techniques on one another.

SECURING COOPERATION
AND STRUCTURING THE INTERVIEW

As ambassadors of the study, interviewers should be trained to be diplomats, particularly when participants are uncooperative or unpleasant. Interviewers are a key reason why participants consent to do an interview and are the main motivator for the way the participants perform their task. The impression that participants have about a study is largely formed by their contact with the interviewers. Participants who do not trust the integrity of the interviewer may refuse to participate or give unreliable answers to the questions.

Interviewer Identification

It is generally not necessary that interviewers immediately show proof of identification when they make contact with a participant. Participants rarely show much interest in badges and hardly ever spontaneously ask for them (Farrington, Gallagher, Morley, St. Ledger, & West, 1990). However, when requested, interviewers should be able to show appropriate credentials, like identification badges with their photograph and the name of the sponsoring institution. It is also handy for interviewers to carry project business cards. These cards can be given to participants for future reference or to individuals who may be able to provide the address of a hard-to-find participant.

Interviewer Dress Code

Participants often consider the interviewer's appearance in deciding to participate in a survey (Singer, 1978). Most studies do not have an explicit dress code, and what is considered appropriate may depend on the kind of participants to be interviewed. Under all circumstances, the interviewers' clothing should be clean, neat, and not offensive. Interviewers should refrain from wearing items like pins and t-shirts that promote political, social, or religious causes. In other words, interviewers should be dressed in such a way that participants are comfortable associating with them.

Initial Interaction With the Participant

The initial interaction of the interviewer with a participant usually determines whether cooperation can be secured. If interviewers make an open-minded and nonjudgmental impression and are trained to have a positive attitude toward people, the respondent most likely will agree to do the interview. Not all participants of a study, however, will be easy to approach. Interviewers should be assured that everybody encounters reluctant participants and that this does not mean they are doing their job badly. Interviewers can be trained to deal with even the most difficult contacting situations through role playing that develops effective dialogue, correct eye contact, and appropriate body movement (Hornik, 1987). Well-trained interviewers who feel optimistic about their ability to persuade respondents to cooperate achieve significantly higher response rates than interviewers who are less optimistic about their contacting skills (Singer, Frankel, & Glassmann, 1983).

Telephone Versus Personal Contact

Some interviewers rely heavily on the telephone whereas others feel more comfortable contacting the participant in person. However, from the participant's point of view, it is much easier to refuse on the telephone than in a face-to-face encounter. Thus, in the first contact, interviewers should be trained to approach a potential participant in person and, in later follow-up, to discontinue the use of the telephone when they sense the slightest reluctance in the participant.

Answering Machines

Many people use an answering machine to routinely screen calls, creating a potential obstacle for interviewers. Owners of answering machines may not readily respond to telephone messages left by an interviewer whose name is not familiar to them. In a nationwide telephone survey, however, Tuckel and Feinberg (1991) showed that a significant portion of people with answering machines could be reached eventually. Answering machines were more of an obstacle during weeknights than on the weekend, when people tended to be at home more and did not turn on their answering machines as often. When encountering an answering machine, interviewers need to be prepared to leave clear and concise messages that state their name, affiliation, and reason for calling, and how they can be reached. Also, they should be trained not to wait too long for an answer but to continue to try contacting the person at different times of the day and different days of the week.

How to Prevent an Outright Refusal

Interviewers should be trained to avoid an outright refusal to participate (Alreck & Settle, 1985). It is much easier to turn around a reluctant participant than to change the mind of a participant who has been given the opportunity by the interviewer to refuse. It should be emphasized during training that, although cooperation rates are important and interviewers are evaluated on the number of refusals they accumulate, it is sometimes necessary to back off from trying to persuade a potential participant to do the interview. It is better to keep the door open for another interviewer to try in the future than to invite a downright refusal and lose any possibility of obtaining the interview. Sometimes it is just not the right time for the participant to be involved in the study. The person may be in the middle of a move, or there may be a death in the family and the participant is not in the mood to answer personal questions. In a study of young women, Robles, Flaherty, and Day (1994) found that resistant participants were significantly more depressed and lived in households that were more often disorganized by serious life events, which may have contributed to their reluctance to be interviewed. It is also possible that interviewers feel that they could not find the right way of interacting with the respondent and that it is better for another interviewer to handle the contact.

In situations where cooperation cannot be obtained immediately, interviewers should be trained to find out the reasons for the reluctance and carefully document all interactions with the participant. Knowing the reasons for the reluctance helps the supervisor in making decisions on how to proceed and will help another interviewer find the right strategies for contacting the participant again at a later date.

Information Concerning the Study

In general, interviewers should know enough of the background of the study to feel comfortable explaining the research project to participants and to answer most questions about it. Interviewers should be prepared to answer such questions as why the participant was selected for the study, who sponsors the study, why the study is being done, and how the information will be used. In longitudinal studies interviewers should also know how to deal with participants who wonder why they are contacted again and why the interviewer cannot do the interview with a neighbor this time.

When providing information about the study, interviewers should keep in mind that participants usually are interested only in a general explanation and tend to forget quickly the goals of the project (Fowler & Mangione, 1990). Most people are not interested in hearing many details about the project. However, if a participant wants to have more information than can be provided, the interviewers should be instructed to say that they do not have this information but that a supervisor will get in touch with the participant as soon as possible.

When explaining the content and goals of the project to the interviewers, the instructors should use the same language that interviewers are expected to use when interacting with the participants. In fact, the terminology should be on the same sixth-grade level that is required for explaining consent. For instance, instead of talking about the development of prosocial and antisocial behavior in children, the instructor may say that the researcher is interested in studying why certain people grow up with problems and why others grow up with none or very few.

It is not necessary for interviewers to be informed about all the hypotheses under investigation. Interviewers who know all the questions that the investigators would like to answer may inadvertently affect the outcome of the study. Their intricate knowledge of the goals of the study may influence the way they ask questions. They may become selective in their handling of probes, or they may become biased in their recording of participants' answers. Even though interviewers may not know all the ins and outs of the study, they should be convinced that they are involved in a worthwhile project.

Specifying the Length of the Interview

While setting up an appointment, the interviewer should discuss with the participant the approximate duration of the interview. Participants do not want their time to be taken for granted. Also, interviewers do not want a participant to walk out on them because the interview was longer than the participant expected. The interviewer should never tell participants that the length of the interview depends on the answers that they give to certain questions. If the participant realizes that answering "no" to lead questions prevents them from having to deal with numerous follow-up questions, the interview may become invalid.

When discussing with the participant the time that needs to be set aside for the interview, the interviewer should also stress the importance of conducting the interview with as few interruptions as possible. Too many delays during the interview because of telephone calls or people walking in and out of the room may make it necessary to continue the interview at a later date, with a chance that it will never be finished.

Interviewing Environment

Although most field interviews are done in the participant's home, this is not always the best place to conduct an interview. In large households a private place to conduct the interview may be hard to find, and it may be problematic to get a participant to cooperate with the interviewer when other occupants of the house, like children, are competing for attention. Also, participants may not like to receive strangers into their homes because they feel embarrassed about their living conditions. It is the interviewer's task to convince the participant of the importance of conducting the interview under the best possible circumstances and discuss the best place for their meeting.

Dining and living rooms are the most common places for in-home interviews. Interviewers should try to sit as closely as possible to participants without invading their personal space. This enables the interviewer to conduct the interview in a low voice, which prevents other people in the home from overhearing the questions. Having a television on usually provides a good sound barrier and helps to create privacy. Participants should have their back turned toward the set so that the interviewers do not have to compete with the television for attention. When children are expected to be a distraction, interviewers may consider bringing coloring books and toys for their entertainment. If there is little chance for privacy inside the house, other possible places to conduct the interview are outside on a porch, the garden, a car, or a nearby public place, like a library.

Explaining the Task of Being Interviewed

The participant is the expert on what the interviewer wants to know but needs to be instructed in his or her role. Participants who understand their role as interviewees will be highly motivated, will try to understand the questions that are being asked, will attempt to retrieve all information that is necessary, and will answer the questions to the best of their ability (Dijkstra, 1987; Fowler & Mangione, 1990).

In preparation for the interview, the interviewer should discuss with the participant the reasons for carrying out the interview in a *standardized* way and the importance of asking questions exactly as worded. Also, informing the participant before the interview that the questions must be asked verbatim will make it more difficult for the interviewer not to do so and thus may increase the standardization of the interview (Fowler & Mangione, 1990).

Participants should be made aware that accurate and complete answers are important. They should also know the format of the answers. If the participants do not have any idea about the kind of answers that are expected, interviewers may find themselves listening to an avalanche of details and sidetracks because the participants believe that the interviewers want as much information as they can muster, whereas, in fact, they need only choose from several answer categories. When participants finally realize that the details are of no importance, they will most likely feel foolish. If the questions require choosing from several answer categories on answer cards, the interviewers should give the participants an example of such a question and demonstrate the use of the answer cards.

Occasionally, participants may challenge interviewers on specific questions or parts of the interview. They may find that a question is badly phrased or not really relevant to the topic under investigation, or they may feel that a different question should have been asked. To avoid lengthy discussions about alternative ways of doing the interview, interviewers may stress the necessity of all participants' answering the same standardized questions while at the same time telling the participants that their comments will be passed on to the investigator.

Maintaining a Professional Relationship

The interviewer should always maintain a professional relationship with the participant in which conducting the interview is the central focus. The most effective way to complete each interview is to combine a friendly attitude with a business sense of purpose. Expressing opinions in response to participants' answers or making spontaneous comments should be avoided. Interviewers should refrain from promoting certain causes, even if it is clear that the participant is in favor of them. They also should not allude to personal experiences or engage in business relations with the participant.

It is usually not a good idea for interviewers to accept offers of food or beverages. It may unnecessarily prolong the time that the interviewer has to spend with the participant and can become distractive to the task at hand. An exception would be if a participant has prepared a special treat in advance, and the interviewer notices that coffee and cookies are on the table. In this situation, the interviewer does not want to offend the participant's offer of hospitality and has to be flexible in dealing with the situation. Offers of alcoholic drinks, however, should be refused under all circumstances. Smoking by interviewers in the homes of participants, even if they smoke themselves, should not be allowed.

Under certain circumstances the behavior of the participant may become unacceptable and the interviewer has to assert control over the situation. For instance, while being interviewed the participant may start playing with a gun or other dangerous weapon or start changing clothes while answering the questions. Interviewers should be taught to ask participants to stop unacceptable behavior or interrupt the interview and leave.

Ending the Interview

Survey research handbooks have paid much attention to gaining cooperation and conducting interviews; in contrast, not much has been written on how to conclude the interview. The interviewers should be trained to leave the participants with a positive feeling about the project. The last impression that the participants have about the interviewer may determine how willing they are to be interviewed again. Because the participant has just spent a sizable amount of time answering questions, some of them personal and of a sensitive nature, it is important that the interviewers give the participants an opportunity to reflect on the interview and ask if they have any questions or comments. The interview booklet should provide for a space to document the participant's observations about the interview to be communicated to the supervisor later. This comment section also can be used to document unusual events that occurred during the interview and that, unlike incidents of child abuse, did not require the immediate action of the office staff. If participants are not paid immediately for their efforts, interviewers should provide clear information about how and when participants will be paid and who to call when problems occur. In addition, participants can be given a card with all the information that they need to contact the study office. This card should include the approximate date that payment can be expected. It goes without saying that the participants should always be thanked for their cooperation.

INTERVIEWING TECHNIQUES

For teaching the interviewing skills discussed below, demonstrations and role playing are very important, and the instructor should be prepared to go through as many exercises as are necessary to transform each trainee into a competent interviewer.

Pacing the Interview

Interviewers vary greatly in their reading styles. Some interviewers are natural readers whereas others administer the interview lifelessly or maintain too fast a pace. If interviewers race through the interview, participants tend to hurry, too. Some interviewers may start to rush the interview because they sense that the participant is becoming impatient; others may become impatient themselves because the interview takes much longer than usual. This situation may lead to the unfortunate pattern of the interviewer asking the next question before the participant has quite finished the previous answer or the participant beginning to answer before the interviewer is finished asking the question. If the interviewer administers the interview too quickly or does not give the participant an adequate time to think about the answers, the participant may conclude that accurate recall and complete answers do not matter. Through role playing, interviewers can be trained to prevent rushing and being rushed and learn to take a break when they feel that they are losing the attention of the participant.

Maintaining Accuracy and Reading Questions as They Are Worded

The uniformity of the data and the validity of the final results of the study depend on the degree of standardization that is maintained in administering the interview. Asking the questions exactly as worded seems an easy skill to teach but is in reality one of the hardest skills for interviewers to maintain. Fowler and Mangione (1990) showed that only 60% of the interviewers with 10 days of training were rated satisfactory or highly satisfactory in reading the questions verbatim. Particularly, interviewers made more reading errors and improvised more frequently in the later part of the interview. Instructors should pay attention to verbatim reading during reading exercises and invite other interviewers to detect any deviations.

Probing

The objective of the interview is to get the participant to answer the questions with responses that fit the answer categories. If the answer is unclear or does not fully constitute an appropriate answer, the interviewer has to probe for an answer that is acceptable or that fits into one of the specified answer categories. The key to good probing is to carefully listen to the participant's attempts to provide the appropriate response and to be able, without becoming directive, to zero in on the fitting answer. Probing is one of the hardest skills for the interviewer to learn and is the greatest source of interviewer error in survey research (Fowler & Mangione, 1990).

The training should ensure that all interviewers *probe in the same way*. As a first technique, the interviewer should be trained to repeat the question. If this does not produce the desired outcome, the interviewer may use other standard probes such as, "Can you tell me more about that?" Interviewers should be trained to mark the questions in the interview that needed probing and indicate how the probing was done. Questions that frequently need probing may have to be treated with some caution in later analyses.

Open-ended questions often require probing. The instructors should provide good examples of fitting answers to open-ended questions so that interviewers know the kind of information that is sought and that can be coded later. If two or more answers for a question are accepted, the number of answers obtained may vary from interviewer to interviewer (Groves, 1989). In training, interviewers should be taught to consistently probe for multiple responses.

The proper use of a "Don't Know" (DK) response to a question needs to be addressed in training. A DK answer may mean that participants claim ignorance, cannot make up their mind, or are not certain about the meaning of the question. Each study may have different definitions of DK answers, and interviewers need to be taught what appropriate use of DKs for a particular study. When probing a DK answer, an interviewer should learn to gauge when additional probing will lead to guesswork on the part of the participant or when the participant will come up with an answer just to please the interviewer.

PRACTICE INTERVIEWS

Practice interviews are the best way to determine whether interviewers are ready to handle their assignments. Several practice interviews in different settings should be completed before the trainee is ready to interview participants. A performance checklist is a handy tool to standardize the evaluation of each practice interview and to document the trainee's progress.

Training Interview

In our study, each interviewer is required, as part of the training, to do a practice interview in which a veteran interviewer plays the role of participant. At the time of the practice interview, the interviewer is expected to be familiar with all parts of the interview and to be able to bring into practice standard interview techniques. Because veteran interviewers are familiar with the questionnaires, they are the ideal mock participants to create difficult skipping patterns, to provide answers that need to be probed, and to set little traps that new interviewers have to resolve. If there are no veteran interviewers, office staff like coders and data analysts familiar with the interview may be used for this purpose.

While the practice interviews are being conducted, the instructors can observe how the new interviewers are handling their task. Based on the instructors' own observations and the evaluation by the veteran interviewers, the instructors can determine whether or not an interviewer is ready to go into the field. Interviewers who receive an unsatisfactory rating are asked to repeat the practice interview at a later date. If their performance is entirely below standard, they can be terminated.

Field Observation Interviews

If veteran interviewers are available, it is useful for trainees to observe a veteran interviewer at work in the field. This can be considered the last step in the training process before interviewers begin to conduct interviews on their own. While observing interviews, the new interviewers can record the answers in the same way as the veteran interviewers and mark questions or areas of the interview that they want to discuss with the veteran interviewer later.

INTERVIEWER BRAINSTORMING

When data collection is in full swing, it is useful to schedule a short additional training session. At this stage of the data collection phase, the interviewer supervisors have a fairly good idea of how the interviewers are dealing with their task. The brainstorming session can be used to fine-tune some of the training techniques and to go over problems that have been noted by the supervisors and the interviewers. It may also function as a booster session for finishing the data collection wave because the later part of a phase is usually more difficult to complete, with more participants being reluctant and interviews becoming harder to schedule. It is important to ensure that the session does not degenerate into bragging about who had the *worst* experience.

Interviewers may want to tell about the house with the most cockroaches, the interview that took three times as long as planned, or the participant who was intoxicated. It is more constructive, instead, to ask each interviewer to relate one of his or her *success stories* such as a unique way of turning around a reluctant participant or a good procedure for engaging a child's attention.

CONCLUSION

Interviewers should be *fully* trained before starting their work in the field. Effective training is best accomplished by preparing a training manual and a detailed training schedule. The training manual should include not only how to deal with participants and how to administer the interview but also the conditions of the job and the legal and technical issues related to being an interviewer. Role playing is an essential part of the training, and interviewers should be tested regularly on the knowledge that they have obtained in class. If instructors are organized and well prepared for the training, interviewers will feel that they should become equally organized and prepared in doing their job. If the instructors show that they care about the quality of the information that will be collected, the interviewers will consider the instructors' example as the standard for their own work. In other words, the instructors prepare interviewers for their task not only by what they teach but also by how they teach.

5

Participant
Acquisition and Retention

Many people are surprisingly willing to be interviewed; consequently, acquiring and retaining participants is, for the most part, not difficult. However, acquiring the *right* participants and *all* the targeted participants is not easy. Nor is it easy to retain all participants over a number of assessments. In this chapter we discuss why high participation and retention rates are important and identify some of the pitfalls in compiling a listing of the population. We also review procedures to optimize participation and retention rates.

PARTICIPATION AND RETENTION RATES

We use the term "participation rate" to refer to the percentage of targeted potential participants who have been inducted into a study. The term "retention rate" refers to the percentage of original participants who take part in a later assessment.

Why a High Participation Rate Is Important

When potential participants are not included in a study because of refusals or the inability to find them, the sample may be biased because different groups of people may have different likelihoods of refusing or of not being found (Bailar, 1989). A biased sample is not representative of the larger population to which the results are meant to apply. Bias in the sample can jeopardize the results in several ways. First, estimates of the occurrence of certain characteristics or conditions in the population may be inaccurate and, consequently, may give an overly optimistic or pessimistic picture of a social problem. This may, for instance, influence the amount of public money set aside to deal with the problem. Second, the relationships between variables under study may be specific to the acquired sample and may suggest conditions related to particular outcomes in people's lives that are relevant only to the biased sample and not to the total population the study was meant to address.

The magnitude of the potential bias in *sample acquisition* is often difficult to evaluate because very little or no information may be available to compare participants with nonparticipants. However, most of the time there is *some* information that may help to evaluate whether the sample is biased. If the addresses of the nonparticipants are known, census data can perhaps be used to estimate socioeconomic characteristics of participants versus nonparticipants. For instance, in our study we found a slight, but nonsignificant, tendency for nonparticipants to live in somewhat better neighborhoods with fewer single-parent households and less neighborhood crime. In addition, if participants are derived from a list of an organization, it may be possible to obtain aggregate data on the whole group of potential participants and compare those with the data from the actual participants. For instance, achievement test results of a sample of school children can be compared with the test results of the whole school district. One should keep in mind, however, that samples can be biased with regard to important dimensions that cannot be measured. This is one of the reasons why it is important to keep participant loss to a minimum.

In initial sample acquisition, it may be possible to replace potential participants who refuse or who cannot be found. However, if the replacements cannot be matched on certain characteristics with the nonparticipants, the problem of potential bias is not addressed and the procedure may only help to preserve the size of the target sample.

Why a High Retention Rate Is Important

As with the initial loss of participants, the danger of attrition in later assessment waves is that the sample will become biased. Generally, studies have found that participants from disorganized families, those who move often, those who are more frequently involved in the use of alcohol or drugs, and those engaged in criminal activities are less likely to be recaptured in follow-ups (Jessor & Jessor, 1977; Nurco, Robins, & O'Donnell, 1977). In our experience, these participants are, indeed, more difficult to *locate*, but they are not more likely to *refuse*. In our study, in which practically all participants are located at every assessment wave and participant refusal is relatively low, we have not found, over six waves, any disproportionate loss with regard to delinquency status, socioeconomic status, race, single parent status, and educational level of the mother. The key is to continue to try to secure an interview because efforts spent in obtaining the interviews from the final participants reduce the possibility of sample bias.

However, even if participant loss is randomly distributed, it can still pose a problem. Consider a data set consisting of five assessment waves. Waves two to five have a 90% participation rate. This does not sound bad until we consider the cumulative effect of nonparticipation. If half of the 10% attrition in each of the waves are always the same participants and the other half refuses only in one wave, then data are incomplete for 25% of the initial participants. This limitation obviously imposes a severe problem for data analysis. Although there are statistical strategies for analyzing data with missing cases (see, e.g., Little & Rubin, 1989), none of them is ideal. Therefore, it is best to try to maximize participation and retention from the start of a study.

How to Assess Participation and Retention Rates

There are many ways of calculating the participation rate, and researchers have some leeway in deciding how to present participant cooperation. Sometimes it is calculated as the number of participants divided by the total number of participants and refusers. A participation rate calculated in this way is *inflated*; it leaves out all potential participants who could not be found or who were hesitant to set up an appointment so that the interview was not done. A more accurate way to calculate a participation rate is to take the ratio of the number of completed interviews to the number of *eligible* persons in the sample. Persons who have died or ineligible people (like girls on a list of boys) should be taken out of the equation. In this way, the participation rate reflects the number of people who participated out of those persons who were targeted and who conceivably could have participated.

It is not always simple, however, to decide whether a person should be taken out of the equation or left in. Some people are very hard to contact, and it may not be clear whether a person is not at home or is not living at the address. Also, if a person does not live at the listed address, it does not necessarily mean that he or she has become ineligible for the study. Some studies allow only a limited number of attempts to contact a person. Once that criterion has been reached, do these people become "failures" or "ineligibles"? We suggest that a person is taken out of the participation rate equation *only if there is positive evidence* that the person should not be included. Thus people who cannot be located are in the equation.

In addition to reporting the participation rate, it also is very useful to indicate how good the initial list of potential participants was, that is, what percentage of the persons on the list were truly possible candidates for the study. The percentage of persons on the list who could not be used may give an indication of how many possible participants were not included in the list. For example, if some subjects on a list that should contain only boys are actually girls, then it is likely that some boys were misclassified as girls and never appeared on the list of boys. Likewise, if many people have moved away, other people, who are not represented on the list, may have moved into the area. Although generally we do not know how many people have been omitted erroneously from a list, the percent of false inclusions may give an indication, and this percentage can be reported.

The calculation of the *retention rate* in follow-up assessments is relatively simple; generally it is calculated as the number of reinterviewed participants divided by the total number of participants in the initial assessment. However, some studies exclude from further participation people who have moved out of a particular area. Some researchers count these persons in the attrition rate, whereas others do not. Similarly, participants who die may or may not be included in the attrition figures. It is best to include everyone in the calculation for retention rate but to break attrition down by source, such as moved, died, refused, or not found. Thus reports of retention rates are meaningful only if the way they are computed is described in terms of what is included and excluded.

What Is a Reasonable Participation Rate?

The requirements for participation in a study and the perceived benefits to the participant, as well as the targeted population, are different from study to study. In some studies, students may be interviewed in school and all that parents have to do is to sign a permission slip. In other studies, delinquency patterns may be followed from one generation to another, and the whole family needs to participate in extensive interviews for a number of years. Mothers of young children are often happy to participate in a study of child development, whereas a study on tax evasion, sexual abuse, or drug dealing may have fewer potential respondents who are eager to participate. Thus the content of the study, the demands on the participant, and other factors have an effect on the participation rate. It is not surprising, therefore, that reports of participation rates vary greatly among research surveys (Capaldi & Patterson, 1987).

Complaints have been voiced in the literature about declining participation rates. We mentioned in Chapter 1 that some investigators blame this trend on the introduction of the informed consent procedure; others blame it on the fact that, with more women working outside the home, it is now more difficult to contact a household. As mentioned in Chapter 4, the use of telephone answering machines has introduced another hurdle. Other reasons that have been alluded to are that people are over-interviewed, that they have been subjected to too much telephone solicitation, or that they have become more suspicious and less willing to let a stranger into their homes (American Statistical Association Conference, 1974; Capaldi & Patterson, 1987; Kalton, 1983; Lavrakas, 1993; Steeh, 1981).

The participation figures that are presented in the literature reflect this pessimism. Kalton (1983) mentions 70%-75% as participation rates for uncomplicated face-to-face interviews, with studies in cities having even lower response rates. According to Capaldi and Patterson (1987), private survey organizations report completion rates on general population surveys averaging 60%-65%, despite three or four callbacks. Their review of follow-up studies noted initial participation rates from 52% to 100%. It is our experience, however, that with good planning and care it is possible for studies to reach participation rates of *at least* 80%.

What Is a Reasonable Retention Rate?

Once the sample is established after the first assessment, what can be expected in terms of the continued cooperation of participants in a follow-up study? As with the initial participation rates, reports of retention rates vary. A low retention rate may result from lack of sufficient information for locating participants, the length of the interval between assessments, the number of required assessments, or participants' views of their past experience with the study.

Miller (1991) quotes low figures for reinterview of around 67% and states that young people, people in large cities, and less affluent people are more mobile, which may influence the ability of a research team to locate participants. Other reviewers of this topic also mention relatively low reinterview rates. Menard (1991) reports some studies with very low retention rates of 50% or less. Capaldi and Patterson (1987), who examined nine follow-up studies, found retention rates from 30% to 80%, with a mean of 62% if the interval between assessments was from 6 months to 2 years. With intervals from 4 to 10 years between assessments the average retention rate was 53%. Retention rates in a review by Cordray and Polk (1983) ranged from 37% to 95%, with a mean of 66%.

These are, on average, somewhat discouraging figures. However, there are enough studies with retention rates in the high 80% or low 90% range, such as the National Youth Survey with 87%, the study conducted by Clarridge, Sheehy, and Hauser with 89% (see Menard, 1991, for both of these studies), and the studies in the Program of Research on the Causes and Correlates of Delinquency with 90% and higher (Huizinga, Loeber, & Thornberry, 1993) to indicate that retention of participants is an appropriate expectation for well-conducted studies. Although adequate preparation, time, and dedication have a lot to do with the final retention rate, the kind of population that is studied—mothers of middle-class preschool children versus homeless men—heavily influence the final rate.

In the remaining sections of this chapter we discuss ways to ensure as much as possible that the eventual sample is representative of the population one has in mind.

ACCURACY OF THE LISTING
OF THE TARGET POPULATION

In Chapter 2 we briefly discussed some of the choices for obtaining a sample and referred the reader to more specialized books and papers. Many strategies for acquiring a sample are predicated on the investigators' ability to obtain a listing of potential participants. Here, we discuss some *practical* issues related to how the listing of the target population (i.e., the sampling frame) is obtained. Questions that should be asked about the listing are: How complete is the listing?; Does it have systematic errors?; and What can be done to reduce these errors ahead of time? The goal is to obtain a listing that is as complete and error-free as possible. Often a listing can be procured that suits one's purpose, such as a list of outpatients of a clinic that treats persons with phobias or a record of all convicted men in a particular jurisdiction. Sometimes cities or utility companies have listings of all addresses, although, of course, their household composition is unknown. However, in other cases, the households are not known and one needs to make a listing of potential participants before the sample can be drawn.

We will treat the formation of a list or pool from which potential participants are selected separately from the actual participant acquisition for the study. It is possible, however, that the identification of potential participants and their interview is done at the same time.

Population Is Known

When starting with a known target population in the form of a list obtained from an organization, such as a school district or a professional organization, one should be alert to potential problems. The list may be inadequate or incomplete, or it may contain errors (Kalton, 1983).

An *inadequate list* may not be intended to cover all possible participants for the planned study. For example, if one is interested in *all* school-age children, a list from public schools in a particular area does not include those students attending parochial or private schools and thus is not representative of all school-age children. Another example is that a list of all subscribers to a public radio station does not contain all persons listening to that station.

An inadequate list may still be the best starting point for assembling a full list. It may be possible to supplement it with lists from other sources. If it is very difficult or costly to obtain a complete list, one may decide to limit the sample population to the inadequate list as long as the incomplete representativeness of the sample is made clear.

Incomplete lists do not contain all possible cases. This may happen if a list is a telephone book or a membership list that is several months old. Lists that are not current have, in addition to omissions, persons who should not be included anymore, such as individuals who have died, who have moved away, or who have discontinued their membership, or for whom the defining characteristics have changed. To reduce errors of exclusion and inclusion of potential participants as much as possible, it is very important to contact potential participants soon after the list is completed.

Even if a list is adequate and complete, it may contain *errors* in the descriptive information of individuals on the list. It may be helpful to know how the list was established to find out how reliable the information is. For instance, if sample selection from a school enrollment list is based on age, it is important to know how dates of birth on the list were obtained. Did the school secretary take the parent's word for it, or did the parent need to show a birth certificate?

Other issues of concern about a list may be whether addresses are kept up to date and whether the list contains aliases or only official names. Persons in charge of maintaining the lists know the strengths and weaknesses of the information but may not volunteer this information unless they are asked directly to point out potential problems. As we mentioned in Chapter 2, criteria for inclusion in a study should always be checked again when a potential participant is contacted to make sure that all participants belong in the study.

Sometimes a list of potential participants may be formed by contacting persons at a place where potential participants are likely to be concentrated rather than by sampling households or using existing lists. This strategy may be used, for example, for a study on the mental health of children with minor physical ailments. In waiting rooms of medical clinics, one could canvass adults who are accompanying children to determine whether the children would qualify for inclusion in the study. This strategy would, of course, be an inadequate coverage of the population of all children because children with no medical insurance may be seriously underrepresented at medical clinics.

Population Is Unknown

A full description of survey sampling when the population is unknown is beyond the scope of this book. However, we will briefly touch on the problems that may be encountered if one needs to do a household sampling for the purpose of making a listing of potential participants to be interviewed at a later date. These potential problems can be divided into problems of *household* coverage and problems of coverage *within households*.

What are some of the common problems one may encounter when trying to identify households? Often, tracts from the latest census are used to identify areas in which households and their occupants will be listed. It is common, however, that new housing developments are not represented in the latest census tracts. Depending on the kind of housing that has been newly built, certain types of persons may be underrepresented. A city may have invested in new housing complexes for poor families, or, alternatively, expensive suburbs may have sprung up, both affecting the distribution of the total population.

In the process of compiling a listing of households, other errors of exclusion may occur. Certain housing units may be easily overlooked, when, for example, a garage or shed is converted into a dwelling or a staircase at the back of a house leads to an occupied basement or attic. The reduction of errors in household coverage depends, to a great extent, on the skill of the enumerator. All possible residences should be systematically searched for, and occupants should be asked a set of carefully worded questions about other households in a building. Signs of nonobvious housing units may be multiple mailboxes, doorbells, names, gas meters, and outside doors.

When a housing unit has been properly identified, within-household errors may still occur. Sometimes, people may not want to disclose the presence of certain individuals in their household. For example, women who are on welfare may not want to disclose the presence of a male friend because the admission of another person who could contribute to the household expenses may alter the woman's benefit status. Sometimes housing units are occupied by more families than is legally allowed (e.g., a daughter and her children have moved in with her mother). Other examples of persons who may not be readily mentioned to an inquisitive stranger are temporarily institutionalized or hospitalized people, illegal immigrants, and persons in hiding who are being sought by the police or by creditors.

It is clear that the persons most easily missed are not randomly distributed across the socioeconomic spectrum. They are less likely to be affluent and are more likely to have been involved in lawbreaking than persons whose occupancy is easily established. Often underreported are young adult males of all ethnic backgrounds, but especially of African American extraction (Bailar, 1989). One of the reasons for this is that a proportion of young adult men may have several residences where they stay temporarily, such as their parents', girlfriends', or friends' homes. None of the occupants of these households may claim this person as a permanent resident. Homeless people are often missed altogether.

Regardless of the method used for determining potential participants in a study, one must be aware of possible flaws in the methods so that remedial action can be taken. If no remedial action can be taken, the goals of the study may need to be narrowed, or, at the very least, the shortcomings of the sample selection need to be clearly described so that the representativeness of the sample can be judged when the results of the study are reported.

HOW TO MAXIMIZE
PARTICIPATION AND RETENTION RATES

After a listing has been obtained and potential participants have been targeted, the aim is to have the largest possible number of targeted individuals participate. At this point, one needs to give serious thought to the questions of why people participate in a study and how a study can be conducted to optimize participation. We will first talk about some general principles and then mention some more specific strategies. Groves, Cialdini, and Couper (1992) have classified the factors that influence participation into societal level factors, attributes of the study, characteristics of potential participants, and attributes of interviewers.

Societal level factors comprise the social responsibility felt by the potential participant but also the number of surveys in which this person has participated, or to which he or she might be exposed in the future. If a person has had few chances to speak his or her mind about societal issues, then participating in a study may be attractive. The perceived legitimacy of a study also falls under this heading. The legitimacy is strengthened when a potential participant knows about important others who are participating, or when the sponsor of the study is seen as a person or organization with authority or prestige.

Next, there are the *attributes of the study* that influence the willingness of a person to participate. These attributes might be the topic, the length of the interview, interview location, and the intrusiveness of the questions. Another consideration is whether the participation of the selected individual is absolutely necessary or whether others can take his or her place. Also included in this category are the perceived benefits to the potential participant, not only in terms of the goals of the study but also in terms of participant remuneration.

Certain *characteristics of the potential participant* may make him or her more or less likely to participate. Some studies have found differential participation rates for older versus younger subjects, between males and females, and for different levels of socioeconomic status (Groves et al., 1992; see also Chapter 3). Physical and mental health problems may influence a person's willingness to be involved in an interview, not only because of fatigue but also because one may be less willing to disclose problems and unhappiness. Other factors that may influence the participation rate are inquisitiveness and the desire to be nice to the interviewer who is nice to you.

There are also temporary characteristics and circumstances that influence participation. Temporary worries, illnesses, disagreements in the household, or being overwhelmed with things to do may coincide with the time that the interviewer contacts the potential participant; these factors may lead to a less than positive reception.

Last, as discussed in Chapters 3 and 4, there are *attributes of the interviewer* that may affect how the potential participant reacts. The sex, age, and race of the interviewers may interact with the participants' views, prejudices, and preferences. The way the interviewer looks, dresses, and speaks, and the way the interviewer tailors the introduction of the study to each individual may be decisive. It is the interviewer's job to be aware of the possible influences on the potential participant's decision to participate and to adjust the interaction to each participant so that he or she is satisfied with taking part in a study. We will now discuss some conditions that may favorably influence participation and retention rates.

Initial Contact With Participants

The first contact with potential participants needs to set the right tone by taking away fears, inspiring the potential participant with trust, and making him or her interested in taking part in the research project. This contact may be in person, as when a household enumeration procedure is used. The enumerator's role, then, is to collect factual information to determine whether there is a qualifying person in the household *and* to set the scene for future cooperation by briefly explaining the rationale for the study. These goals may have to be accomplished while standing at the door, or worse, talking through an intercom.

The situation of a recruiter in a place where potential participants converge, as in a clinic, may be better. The recruiter is in a professional environment and obviously must have the permission of the clinic administration to recruit participants.

Let us now consider the situation in which a listing of possible participants has been obtained and an interviewing phase is about to begin. It is a good idea to inform potential participants by mail ahead of time that someone will be contacting them. Such a letter should be brief and relatively simple in language. The letter should be on official letterhead, preferably that of a recognized organization, like a university or a hospital known to the potential participants. The content should cover the goal of the study, why this particular person was selected (random, member of a group, etc.), how his or her name was obtained, remuneration, and when and how the potential participant will be contacted.

Confidentiality of the information gathered in the interview should be stressed. This is especially important if the individual's name was obtained from an organization with which the potential participant might have an antagonistic relationship (e.g., when the association between the individual and the organization is mandated by a court as in the case of imprisonment or treatment for sexual or drug abuse). If there is no reason to expect an antagonistic relationship, it may be helpful to have the organization that provided the names cosign the letter or send a brief letter in support of the study on its own letterhead.

Initial letters are also useful vehicles for updating addresses before interviewers try to contact potential participants. For this purpose, envelopes should be marked "address correction requested." Enough time should be allowed for address corrections to be returned to the office by the postal service.

Interviewers should not be surprised if potential participants do not remember receiving the introductory letter or do not remember its content. It is good practice to re-supply a copy of the letter to potential participants to refresh their memory or to establish the interviewer's legitimacy, if necessary.

Participant Remuneration

The topic of many studies may be vaguely interesting or beneficial to respondents, but usually not to the extent that they feel gratified by just participating. Therefore, it may be necessary to compensate participants for their *expert information* and for the *time* they set aside for the interview. The compensation may take the form of gifts or money. Gifts represent an immediate, concrete reward for participating in the study. Also, gifts can be targeted specifically for the participants, thus increasing the likelihood that they, and not their family members, primarily enjoy the reward. For instance, monetary rewards for a child participant may be used by the caretaker to pay bills, whereas a gift like a small portable radio is more likely to stay with the child. On the other hand, not everyone may like a particular gift and some persons may prefer receiving money. In longitudinal studies, a system of gradually increasing payments, outlined in the consent form, may encourage respondents to continue with the study until the end.

Some projects make cash payments right after completion of the study protocol. This procedure is most rewarding to the participant, but some organizations may not allow their staff members to carry large sums of money and interviewers may not feel safe walking around with cash. An alternative is to mail checks or, in some cases, money orders when the interview is completed. If participant remuneration is sent by mail, it is important that this is handled by the project staff and not, for instance, by an administrative or fiscal office of a university. Mail may be undeliverable and does occasionally get lost. Project office staff can respond promptly and courteously to queries about payment, whereas questions about checks may not get the same attention from an office that has no direct interest in the success of the study.

Aside from the agreed upon remuneration, it may be possible to occasionally give participants an extra, *noncontingent* gift. Many organizations are willing to provide small gifts for free. Most professional and college sports teams have blocks of free tickets, photographs, and stickers; fast food outlets may give coupons for free drinks or food; publishing houses may have books they would like to donate; and so on. Even though the dollar value of such gifts may be small, getting something free appeals to most participants of any age. It is important, however, to select *neutral* presents and not things that may offend certain categories of participants. Items with political or religious connotations are inappropriate.

Each investigator needs to check with the local Institutional Review Board to determine what an allowable remuneration is. Some IRBs have objected to remunerations as being too large and, therefore, coercive. Our own opinion is that considering what study participation requires in time and invasiveness, but particularly taking into account that the participants are the *experts* on what the researcher wishes to know, they should be adequately rewarded.

Mailings

Frequent mailings also help to build a positive relationship with participants. Aside from letters announcing new assessment phases, mailings can include cards confirming appointments, thank-you letters accompanying payments, and additional thank-you letters at the end of each assessment phase, as well as birthday cards, season's greetings, letters of condolence, and newsletters about the study. Modern software packages with graphics and newsprint capabilities make the design of cards, newsletters, and certificates a desktop job. The mailings also permit the updating of addresses, if address corrections are requested.

Ease of Participation

To maximize cooperation, participation should be made as easy as possible. Unless complicated equipment is required or a standardized environment is necessary, interviewers should be flexible about the time and the location of interviews; the interviews should be done *when* and *where* it is most convenient for participants, as long as the quality of the assessment and privacy can be ensured.

Experience With Previous Interviewer(s)

In later assessment phases of an ongoing study, willingness to continue participation depends to a large extent on the participant's experience with the previous interviewer(s). The participant may consider being interviewed again if previous interviewers were courteous, the interviews were not too long, the questions were not painful or embarrassing, and the remuneration was worthwhile. It is, therefore, crucial for the interviews to be conducted in a professional and pleasant manner. Aside from random checks on interviewers' behavior in the field during an assessment phase, it is also worthwhile to check the long-term effect of interviewers on refusals. The use of coercive techniques may lead to participation in one phase of the study but may result in refusal and resentment in a later phase.

Clear Consent Forms

Consent forms are a help rather than a hindrance to soliciting participation. In our experience, very few people refuse to participate at the time that interviewers present them with the consent form because all points covered in that document should already have been explained and questions should have been resolved. A well-written consent form, in language that participants understand, can be a great help in ensuring continuing participation. It is often reassuring to potential participants to see everything spelled out on paper.

When future assessments are listed clearly, participants know what they have committed themselves to and will not be surprised or annoyed when they are contacted again. If a consent form requests permission for only one assessment but the investigator has made preliminary plans for future assessments, it is important to let participants know that they may be contacted again. Participants may be annoyed when recontacted if they were under the impression that they had committed themselves to one interview only.

SEARCHES AND RELUCTANT PARTICIPANTS

Once every effort has been made to optimize the general conditions for participation and retention, there are still two specific tasks to accomplish to ensure high cooperation rates. The participation rate ultimately depends on the time and effort spent on making sure that all participants are *located* and on *convincing* reluctant people to take part in the study.

Search Techniques

The task of locating individuals is usually most difficult at the first assessment when often the only information one has is the names and addresses of potential participants. In later assessments more information may be available to aid in searching for participants. We first discuss the preparations that can be made to gather information to locate participants, after which we discuss a plan of action for searches.

If a listing of potential participants is to be obtained from an organization for participant acquisition, it is helpful to request that the listing contain more than just names and addresses. Names of relatives, a person's profession and Social Security number, and other similar data can all help to locate someone. It is possible, though, that organizations may not wish to divulge so much information from their files. However, they may be willing to assist if there is a problem locating a potential participant.

There are several general principles for building up information to facilitate searches for later assessments. The groundwork for successful searching for participants is established in the consent form by asking permission from the participant to request new addresses from places of employment, schools, or institutions. This allows access to sources of information that would be unavailable without proof of permission from the participant to divulge information about him or her.

At every assessment wave, information should be gathered about whether the participant plans to move and about names and addresses of friends and relatives who always know the respondents' whereabouts. In addition, in all correspondence, participants should be asked to contact the project if they have moved, if their telephone number has changed, or if they are difficult to reach. In one of our studies about 2.5% of our sample responded to this request. Although this seems a low percentage, it constituted about 14% of the potentially difficult to contact cases and represented a considerable saving in search time.

The final general principle sounds terribly simple: Collect identifying information as *much* and as *often* as possible. Seemingly factual information such as names, birthdays, addresses, Social Security numbers, and family relationships sometimes turns out to be surprisingly inaccurate or fleeting. For instance, participants may have a bewildering variety of names and aliases. A child may be listed on his birth certificate as Napoleon Augustus Jones, but Mr. Jones, Sr., may have disappeared soon after Napoleon's birth and the child may have used the mother's maiden name or last names of mother's boyfriends. Alternatively, he may hardly know what his real name is because everybody calls him Skinny Beanstalk, or Esbe for short. It is important to keep up to date with all names and aliases because the participant may be known by different people or organizations under different names.

It is useful to develop a systematic procedure for locating cases. As an example we will describe the steps we use in searching for participants. Compared to other cities, Pittsburgh has a stable population. Still, within each 6 months, 15% to 18% of the families in our sample move, albeit most of the moves are within the city. Because all assessments for an interview wave in our study are compressed into 3 months, searching for families has to be undertaken without delay and with vigor.

About 25% of the people who move are found simply by requesting address corrections when sending mail. If mail comes back undeliverable and without a new address, interviewers follow standard procedures to locate the participant. The interviewers must consult the telephone book and directory assistance and must find out as much information as possible at the *site of the last known residence*. When interviewers go to the old, and presumably incorrect, address, they sometimes find the participant still there. If the person no longer lives at the address, a current resident, the building manager or owner, a local store clerk, or a neighbor may know where the participant has moved or may be able to direct the interviewer to someone who may know where the participant is. Because interviewers want to proceed with their cases quickly, they are inclined to solve problems themselves. In our experience, interviewers solve about 25% of all search problems.

If the interviewers' search efforts have proven to be unsuccessful, they turn the search problem over to office staff. The office staff uses information that is not accessible to interviewers because of its potential to influence the interviewer's view of the participant.

The first avenue of inquiry attempted by the office staff is the telephone numbers of friends and relatives provided by participants in previous interviews. Use of this information solves about 6% of the search cases. However, participants who move often and are somewhat disorganized may not inform others about their moves or may have friends and relatives who, themselves, move often.

Contacting organizations and agencies for information about participants is also the task of the office staff. This is done to streamline inquiries. Because most organizations are under no obligation to divulge information, a positive relationship with agency personnel needs to be *fostered* so that they are willing to find information and to release it in a timely manner. Recently, CD-ROM telephone directories have become available, facilitating nationwide searching for telephone numbers.

The office staff also reads previous interviews to find clues about the person's whereabouts. Professions, memberships in organizations, serious medical conditions, and unusual hobbies may form starting points for a search. For children, one of the best sources for a new address is their last known school. As a rule, schools are able to give the name and address of the school to which a student has moved so that the new school can be contacted to trace the child's whereabouts. In our study, about 22% of hard-to-find cases are solved this way.

The remainder of searches are solved with the help of employers, child protection agencies, welfare authorities, the military, housing authorities, the department of motor vehicles, and probation or social work departments. Social Security numbers and, for adult populations, driver's licenses are important tools for tracking.

There are agencies that, for a fee, track persons. These agencies use a large number of databases (e.g., Thomas, 1990), and their services can be accessed by computer. Before engaging an agency it is important to find out what databases they use to determine whether the search will be helpful. In our experience tracking agencies are particularly useful for those people who are easiest to find, such as people who have a credit history, who obtain a new driver's license when they move to another state, have a bank account, and have a telephone. Current information on people with fewer ties to the middle class may not show up in electronic databases.

Because searching can take a long time and most search attempts are unsuccessful, it is important to try many avenues simultaneously, even the most unlikely ones, and not give up. When every method for finding a person has been tried without success, the only option is to *start all over again*. In the meantime a relative may have heard about the family in question, a phone may be reconnected, a probation officer may know that the participant is in jail, or a school may have a new address. Although *practically all participants can be found*, searching can be time-consuming and frustrating. We have found it helpful to discuss outstanding cases at a weekly meeting, to rejoice in the solved cases, and to brainstorm for ideas for the unsolved cases.

A word of caution should be inserted about what methods should be used to locate participants. There are illegal ways to obtain information about participants. *Never* should staff be allowed to pursue any method of obtaining information that is illegal or that makes use of false pretenses.

Refusals and Postponements

Once a person has been located, there may still be some hurdles to overcome before an interview can take place. A participant may decide not to take part in the study or may not make up his or her mind. However, there are many reasons for refusals that the interviewer can address to the satisfaction of the participant. In our experience, about *half* of the people who at one time say that they do not want to do an interview later readily consent to be interviewed. It is, therefore, important that interviewers, when encountering resistance, always leave the door open for a future contact. Once a person has decided not to participate, it is always necessary to *ask permission for further contacts*. Most of the time this permission is granted.

Another source of loss occurs at the end of an interviewer phase; it may not have been possible to schedule an interview in time, or the person may not have made up his or her mind to participate prior to the deadline. This may happen if the interview phase was too short, if an interviewer did not try hard to obtain the interview, or if temporary problems experienced by the potential participant, like illness, prevented the interview from being scheduled. Putting a ceiling on the number of contacts to be made for each potential participant (as survey organizations often do) also may result in this type of participant loss.

To achieve a high participation rate, one should be prepared to spend a long time and considerable resources on the last 10% of the sample. In one of our studies it took interviewers a little over 2 weeks to complete interviews with 90% of the resident biological fathers; however, the completion of the remaining 10% took over 7 weeks (Stouthamer-Loeber, van Kammen, Loeber, Miller, & Kumer, 1992). In terms of number of contacts or attempts to contact, 90% of the sample required 7 attempts or fewer, whereas the remaining 10% required up to 24 attempts to contact. If one allows sufficient time for the final stretch and one can muster financial resources, creativity, persistence, and good humor, it is possible to achieve high participation and retention rates.

CONCLUSION

A positive, problem-solving outlook, combined with a sharp eye for possible problems as well as for opportunities to improve the listing of potential participants, participant acquisition, and participant retention, is necessary for the success of a study. High participation and retention rates reduce the possibility of potential bias in the results of the study. Although the procedures mentioned in this chapter have proven to be useful, it is important to be creative because each study has its own restrictions, but also its own opportunities, for locating participants and engaging them in a study. Even though participation and retention rates of other studies cannot be used as exact yardsticks for one's own study, the knowledge that there are studies that achieve high participant cooperation can be an energizing force in trying to reduce participant loss.

6

Supervision of Interviewers

Supervision of interviewers may be best described as providing solution-oriented support while at the same time insisting on a strict adherence to the rules. Effective supervision ensures that interviews are of high quality, participants are located, and refusals are kept to a minimum. Successful supervision hinges on a timely exchange of information between interviewer and supervisor. Interviewers need to be in regular contact with their supervisors to hand in completed interview materials and receive new cases; they need to brainstorm about problems and receive instructions on how to proceed with particular participants. Supervisors need to be in regular contact with interviewers to be kept informed about what is going on in the field; they need to know whether interviewers are progressing with their work as expected and how they can assist interviewers in their efforts. Frequent interaction between interviewer and supervisor prevents problems from accumulating or from being set aside until they hamper the progress of the study or until it becomes too late to take action.

Setting realistic standards for quantity and quality of the interviewers' work is the key to successful supervision; interviewers will be productive, and are likely to try harder, when they feel that they can meet the supervisor's demands. If performance standards are set too high, interviewers may lose interest and feel that the system is to blame for the fact that they cannot keep up with the requirements of the job. If standards of employment have to be revised in midstream to prevent the project from being in danger of losing too many interviewers, interviewers may feel that standards really do not matter and that expectations do not have to be fulfilled (Peters & Waterman, 1982).

This chapter deals with the supervision of interviewers who work outside of the office, but many of the procedures that are related to the monitoring of production and the quality of the interviews apply to in-house interviewing as well. We discuss how to keep the interviewer and the supervisor organized, how to keep track of the interviewing progress, how to maintain quality control, and how to reduce the pool of interviewers when closing out an assessment phase. We stress the importance of visibly demonstrating the progress in an assessment phase and of integrating quality control procedures on a routine basis.

Establishing an appropriate supervision format depends largely on the particular features of the study. In our experience, the best format is regular one-on-one meetings between the supervisor and the individual interviewer rather than group meetings, for the following reasons. First, in one-on-one sessions each individual interviewer can be given more focused attention. Second, confidential information about participants that does not concern other interviewers may have to be discussed in supervision. Third, a group meeting has the potential to become more of a social event than a work-related problem-solving session. However, individual sessions may not always be possible. A study office located in a town other than where the interviewing takes place will limit the time that supervisors are able to meet with interviewers face-to-face. Under such circumstances, supervision may have to be done in weekly group meetings or in a combination of group meetings and individual telephone supervision. If interviewers are dispersed over a large geographical area, supervision may have to be done entirely by telephone, fax, or e-mail. The experiences described in this chapter are based on face-to-face individual supervision, but most of the information also applies when other supervision methods are used. Whatever supervision mode is used, supervisors should allow interviewers enough time to communicate their experiences and provide them with support to overcome existing obstacles and to tackle new problems. The objective of the supervision structure is to support interviewers in doing their jobs and to recognize problems as early as possible so that immediate action can be taken.

THE SUPERVISION STRUCTURE

Interviewers should be expected to attend supervision sessions regularly, preferably once a week, at a set time. Adhering to regular supervision sessions should be part of the contract that interviewers sign when starting their employment. Scheduling supervision at set times gives the interviewers a clear message that they are expected to work continuously on their cases and cannot slack off for a couple of weeks without it being noticed. Even if interviewers have not completed any cases in the previous week, they should be required to meet with their supervisor and discuss the status of their work. Missing or trying to postpone weekly supervision is often an indication that interviewers are not following up on their cases. Supervisors should document how regularly interviewers attend supervision. The attendance record should be part of the interviewer's evaluation. A poor attendance record can be grounds for dismissal or negatively influence the decision of whether to rehire an interviewer for a later assessment wave.

There is also a need to have a format to communicate regularly with the interviewers when they are away from the office. Because interviewers spend a great deal of time in the field and often have other jobs, attempts to get in touch with them can be time-consuming and frustrating. As a solution, an answering machine is used in our study to transmit daily messages between interviewer and supervisor. Interviewers are required to call the supervisor's answering machine *every day* to receive and relay information. In this way, supervisors can pass on general messages that need all interviewers' immediate attention as well as specific information for individual interviewers, such as new addresses for an outstanding case or a participant's request to change the time of the interview. Also, the interviewers, without having to reach the supervisor, can leave messages on the answering machine. For instance, they may need the supervisor to obtain clearance for an interview to be conducted in prison, or they may need some additional information on the whereabouts of a participant.

The answering machine can also be used to report on scheduled and completed cases so that the office is provided with the most up-to-date information on the field effort at all times. Keeping track of the day-to-day progress of the interviewers can be particularly useful in studies that are in the process of selecting their sample. Knowing at all times that interviews are scheduled and completed enables the investigator to terminate quickly and effectively the contacting of new participants if a quota has been reached.

For the answering machine to be an effective tool, it is imperative that interviewers listen to the answering machine when required and that supervisors know who has called. Therefore, interviewers should always leave a record of their call on the answering machine, even when they have nothing to communicate to the supervisor.

Although we rely on the answering machine as a mode of communication, the same can be achieved by using fax or e-mail. These methods require interviewers to own, or at least have access to, fax machines or computers with modems. All of these systems leave a record of the interaction between supervisors and interviewers; however, fax and e-mail records are more easily accessible for visual inspection.

KEEPING TRACK OF THE FIELD EFFORT

An efficient system of tracking the field effort is indispensable for the supervision of interviewers. Without such a system, supervisors will not be able to review quickly the interviewers' work and the progress of the assessment phase. Thus they will not be able to take timely action when the field effort needs to be redirected.

Monitoring Contacts With Participants

Before the start of a data collection phase, a form should be generated for each participant. To distinguish this form from other forms we call this a contact sheet. One function of the contact sheet is to relay basic information for contacting a participant, like an identification number, the participant's name and aliases, names of other members in the household and their relationship to the participant, address, telephone number(s), and the target date of the case. In our study, each address also has a grid location, linked to a street map that is used by the interviewers. The grid locator allows addresses to be found quickly and has the added advantage that respondents who live close together (in a particular grid or series of grids) can be assigned to the same interviewer.

The second function of the contact sheet is to keep track of all field and office efforts related to obtaining and completing the case. Figure 6.1 is an example of how a contact sheet may be filled out. For each contact, the interviewer records the date, the day of the week, and the time of day. The interviewer also records the method of contact, such as telephone, letter, or house contact, and the individual with whom the interviewer talked. For instance, interviewers may record whether they talked to the actual participant or to another person, like a grandmother or an uncle in the household.

The documentation of contacts enables the supervisor to evaluate how diligently the interviewers are working on their cases. Ineffective patterns of contacting are easily detected from the documentation, and a different plan of action may be suggested. The supervisor may advise that the interviewer try to reach a participant on other days of the week or different hours of the day. Another suggestion may be for the interviewer to make home visits when telephone contacts have failed. For later reference, the supervisor should keep a record of these directives as notes in the computerized tracking system that is explained later

```
INTERVIEWER: _____          PHASE 1N              SUBJ:    9999
                             CONTACT SHEET
JOHN GOODFRIEND
IMA GOODFRIEND (BIO. MOTHER)
999 MAIN STREET    843
PITTSBURGH, PA 15213
GRID LOCATION 12L
                             NEW ADDRESS: _____
PHONE 1:   (412)-123-4567
PHONE 2:                                  _____

TARGET DATE:  03/12/94       NEW PHONE: _____
```

DAY/WK	DATE	TIME	NOTES	CODE
Tues	03/09/94	1200	Participant - no answer (house)	03
Tues	03/09/94	1900	Daughter- call back later at 2230 (phone)	34
Wed	03/10/94	1600	Participant - App. sched. for 3/13/94 at 0900 (phone)	36
Sat	03/13/94	0900	Participant - Interview completed (house)	10
Tues	03/16/94	1100	Interview turned in to office	12
Fri	03/19/94	1315	Interv. returned to interviewer for corrections	11
Sat.	03/20/94	1100	Participant - no answer (phone)	33
Sat.	03/20/94	1300	Participant; made corrections (phone)	13
Tues	03/23/94	1100	Interview resubmitted	15
Sat.	04/15/94	1100	Interview completed	01

REASON OR REFUSAL: _____

Figure 6.1. Contact Sheet

in this chapter. In subsequent supervisions, the directives can be reviewed and other directives can be provided if necessary.

Recording search attempts should be a part of the contact sheet documentation and should include even the most insignificant search effort, like calling directory assistance for a new telephone number. When contacting neighbors, interviewers should document as accurately as possible whom they contacted, where this person was located, and what transpired in the contact. If an interviewer search proves to be unsuccessful and is taken over by a supervisor, complete and detailed documentation makes it possible to ascertain what was tried already, in which order, and at what time. The supervisor will continue to document additional search efforts to keep the documentation complete. This documentation can be accomplished by continuing to record searches on the same contact sheet or by using a separate contact sheet if some contacts involve information that the supervisor does not want to share with the interviewer to prevent bias. An example may be a contact with a former parole officer or a shelter facility.

The contact sheet should remain with the interview schedule until the interview is fully completed and checked. If interview schedules have missing or incomplete data and participants have to be contacted again to obtain additional information, the interviewers also record these interactions with respondents on the contact sheet. Thus, in the end, there is a complete overview of the total contact and search efforts for each individual case.

A third important aspect of the contact sheet documentation is the recording of refusals. If an interviewer is not able to convince a respondent to participate, the reason for the refusal should be recorded in as much detail as possible. When, at a later stage, another interviewer is assigned to the case, this information is the starting point for developing a strategy that will turn around the reluctant respondent.

Contact sheets should be considered part of the data and returned to the interviewers for corrections when omissions or errors are found. If the contact documentation is accurate, the record of contacts can form the basis for estimating the total effort of completing the data collection and can assist researchers in the planning of future interviews. For instance, the average amount of contact time may be used to determine the level of pay for interviewers. A complete record of contacts can also serve as a reference tool to search for participants in later phases.

Computerized Tracking System

To supervise a large field staff that is conducting a sizable number of interviews in a short period of time, we, like other researchers (e.g., Karweit & Meyers, 1983), have developed a computerized system that keeps track of the field effort. It is not difficult to set up such a system. All that is required is data management software, some programming skills, and above all, knowing what needs to be tracked.

A good tracking system should be able to answer general questions related to the progress of data collection as well as specific questions concerning interviewers and interviews. The system should be able to determine whether the data collection phase is proceeding according to schedule, whether the performance of one interviewer differs from the rest of the interviewing team, and which cases are lagging behind in being completed. A central component of the system is the tracking of the most up-to-date status of each case. This means that a record is maintained to indicate not only whether or not a case was completed but also whether the interview materials were passed on to the office, interview schedules were checked for completeness, corrections were made, and so on. Materials like interview booklets, which are processed by a number of people and are frequently moved between offices, can easily be misplaced. Knowing exactly where interview materials should be makes it easier to find the materials in case they are temporarily lost.

For cases that are in the process of being scheduled, the system should keep a record of the interactions between the interviewer and the participant so that the supervisor can draw inferences about each outstanding case without having to consult an interviewer. For instance, the supervisor may conclude that an interviewer contacted a participant for the first time 4 weeks earlier and scheduled an appointment in the following week, which was subsequently broken but not yet rescheduled. By maintaining a record of the field effort, problems with a case such as a lack of effort in pursuing a participant can be easily spotted and addressed with the interviewer during supervision.

The tracking system can also monitor participant payments. When participants are reimbursed by check, the system should track not only whether the study office sent a check to the participant but also whether a check was received for payment by the bank. Participants sometimes forget to cash their checks or, worse, do not receive them at all. The tracking system prevents having to go through piles of cancelled checks and thus enables the study to respond quickly if a payment problem occurs. A similar strategy can be used for keeping track of interviewer payments.

If assessments need to be completed at regularly spaced intervals, the tracking system should include the date that cases are targeted for completion. The system may also include the date that the case was assigned to an interviewer so that cases that have been in the hands of an interviewer too long can be easily identified.

Monitoring Interviewers' Performance

To make optimal use of the time allotted for supervision, the computerized tracking system can generate for each interviewer an up-to-date performance report that highlights the issues that need to be discussed during supervision. This report includes statistics on completed interviews and refusals as well as a list of outstanding cases. Interviews that require special attention, like cases that have overdue target dates or have been in the interviewer's hands for too long, are flagged to alert the supervisor that the progress on these cases needs to be addressed.

During supervision, the current status of each case is added to the tracking system. At the same time, suggestions and new plans of action are recorded. Figure 6.2 is an example of how an interviewer tracking sheet can be used to summarize what is going on with each outstanding case. It contains the updated and previous status codes of each interview, the date of issue, the target date, and the supervisor's comments. Cases that are completely finished no longer show up on the tracking sheet, whereas the ID numbers of newly assigned cases appear for the first time. The tracking sheet is signed by both the interviewer and the supervisor and functions as an official record of the contacts that are in the hands of the interviewer. A copy of the tracking sheet with the suggestions made during the supervision is given to the interviewer and can serve as a reference tool for future actions.

Assigning Cases

Interviewers should have a limited number of cases to work on to avoid the situation in which only easy-to-schedule cases are completed and more difficult contacts are ignored and left to accumulate. The number of assigned cases may differ from study to study and may depend on how many interviews can be completed between supervisions. In our project, which averages about three interviews per interviewer each week, interviewers usually do not have more than ten contact sheets in their hands at any given time. This does not include completed cases that were returned to the interviewer for corrections and that may involve re-contacting a participant.

How hard interviewers have worked in the previous week should determine whether or not their workload will be increased or decreased. Assigning new cases should depend not only on the interviewers' number of completed cases in the previous week but also on how actively they have worked on cases that are still outstanding. In other words, based on previous performance, the supervisor decides whether interviewers will be assigned more cases or whether some of their contacts will be taken back and distributed to other interviewers.

TRACKING SHEET----SPRING 94   PAGE 1

PREPARED ON 04/01/94   INTERVIEWER: 205

ID_S	WEEK 1	WEEK 2	WEEK 3	WEEK 4	ISSUED	TARGET
10100					04/01/94	04/21/94
	JUST ASSIGNED					
10213		33	03	36	03/11/94	04/10/94
	SCHEDULED 4/7/94 NEEDS CONSENTS					
11555	03	03	03	73	03/04/94	04/06/94
	PEOPLE NOT LIVING THERE/WILL GO TO NEIGHBORS					
12056	34	36	10	11	03/04/94	*****
	BACK FOR CORRECTION					
13415	03	34	34	35	03/04/94	04/07/94
	PARTICIPANT HESITANT ON PHONE/DO HOME VISIT					
13567			04	19	03/18/94	04/16/94
	PARTICIPANT IN HOSPITAL/WAIT TWO WEEKS BEFORE CONTACT					
14218			36	12	03/18/94	*****
	INTERVIEW TURNED IN TO OFFICE					

You will be paid based on completed interviews as indicated above. If any modifications need to be made because of improperly filled-out questionnaires, you will be notified as soon as possible.

_____   _____
INTERVIEWER SIGNATURE   SUPERVISOR SIGNATURE

Figure 6.2. Tracking Sheet

Review of Progress

The progress of the assessment phase should be reviewed on a regular basis. With little effort, the computerized tracking system can produce a status report with all the pertinent information to evaluate how well data collection is proceeding. The first part of the report used in our weekly staff meeting includes general statistics on the total number of completed interviews, refusals, searches, overdue cases, and cases that have been outstanding for longer than 4 weeks. Further, this part of the report also includes the number of interviews for which data have been entered by the office. Based on this information, the staff can decide whether more attention should be paid to searches, overdue interviews, or refusals. If the number of interview booklets processed by the office lags behind the number of incoming interviews, staff may be reallocated temporarily to catch up with the data entry and checking of interview materials. If the rate of completion of interviews is very much lower than expected, the investigator may even consider hiring and training more interviewers.

The second part of the progress report categorizes information by individual interviewer. It includes the number of completed cases, scheduled interviews, finished cases that need corrections, and refusals. This part of the report is the basis for the weekly evaluation of each interviewer. It enables the staff to recognize outstanding performance and also to make decisions about interviewers who are not completing enough cases or have incurred too many refusals. When, toward the end of the interview phase, the workload decreases and less interviewing staff is needed, the progress report is indispensable in deciding who should be retained and who should be laid off.

In the third part of the weekly report, problem cases are identified by category and listed with an overview of what has been done to complete these cases over the previous weeks. Outstanding searches are a particularly important category of problem cases, and a substantial part of the weekly progress review is devoted to brainstorming for new ways of finding lost participants. Other sections may document the progress of contacting out-of-town participants, overdue cases, or reluctant participants.

QUALITY APPRAISAL

Because interviewers work mostly independently, the temptation to deviate from the rules is considerable and clearly necessitates a system of continuous and vigilant checking. Researchers may feel ambivalent about checking the quality of the interviewers' work and be reluctant to institute a system of close monitoring because they may feel that it will project an atmosphere of distrust of their staff. Investigators may argue that interviewers are professionals and, therefore, are expected to do a good job. However, just as car manufacturers are expected to check the proper installation of brakes and pharmaceutical companies are expected to check that the bio-availability of the drug is the same from medication batch to medication batch, researchers also should be expected to check the quality of their data so that statements resulting from their study are not misleading because of sloppy data collection. It is not enough to believe that interviewers will never be inattentive, take shortcuts, or cheat. It is better to have proof that this is, indeed, the case. If close quality control is well planned and implemented right from the beginning of the study, the staff will see it as part of the regular routine and nobody will feel singled out for special scrutiny. Close monitoring also provides an opportunity to detect improvement and outstanding performance for which interviewers should be given recognition. The following sections will describe several methods for ensuring the quality of the data collected in the field.

Field Observations

Accompanying interviewers in the field is the most immediate way to evaluate their performance. By directly observing the interview, the supervisor can ascertain whether questions and instructions are read verbatim, skipping patterns are followed, and correct probing techniques are used. If the supervisor also writes down the respondent's answers, the recordings of the interviewer can be compared later with those of the supervisor to determine whether the two sets of recordings are consistent with each other and thus establish reliability of the interviewer's recording. If this method of observation is used, the interviewers should make sure that the participant clearly understands that the supervisor is not present to evaluate the performance of the participant but to make sure that the interviewer is doing a good job.

Special attention should be paid to the interviewer's interactions with the participant before, during, and after the interview. Especially in longitudinal studies, continued cooperation depends, to a certain extent, on the participant's experience with the previous interviewer(s). If an interviewer was courteous and conducted the interview in a professional manner, the participant may consider being interviewed again. On the other hand, discourteous interviewers may have a negative effect on the willingness of participants to be further involved in the study.

Observation interviews screen out those interviewers who have trouble with the administration of the interview or who need to improve their interactions with the participant. Observing the interviews also gives the interviewers the message that standardization really matters (Fowler & Mangione, 1990), which can have a positive effect on their overall performance (Billiet & Loosveldt, 1988).

Tape Recording Interviews

Another way of monitoring the interviewers' performance is to tape record the interviews. If feasible, the investigator may decide to have every interview recorded but to select only certain interviews to be checked later. This strategy has the advantage of making interviewers feel that they always have to be on their best behavior because they never know which interviews will be evaluated.

Although the tape recording of interviews is an effective way to evaluate whether the interviewers ask questions verbatim and in the right order, this method of quality control has drawbacks. Some participants do not like to be audiotaped, especially when the questions are sensitive; as a consequence, the way participants answer the questions may be negatively affected. Tape recording fails to show important aspects related to conducting an interview such as eye contact, facial expression, and other body language. Also, answers given in a nonverbal manner are not recorded. These problems could be eliminated by videotaping the interviews, but this solution would be very cumbersome and even more intrusive than tape recording.

Interviewing a "Phantom" Participant

The majority of the interviewers conduct interviews according to the rules when their supervisor is present or when they are asked to tape record the interview. Unfortunately, this does not mean that interviewers always conduct interviews in the same correct manner when they are not directly monitored. To try to safeguard against this possibility, a "phantom" participant may be inserted into the participant pool (see also Alreck & Settle, 1985). This person is not a participant but, rather, is specially employed by the project to give feedback on interviewers' performance. Interviewers will not know whether they are interviewing a "real" participant or the imposter, and the knowledge of the existence of a "phantom" participant may prevent them from deviating from the rules.

Interview Verifications

After the interview is completed, the interviewers' performance should be checked by randomly calling or visiting about 10% of the participants. Preferably, the person responsible for the interview verification should work *independently* from the supervisors and report directly to the senior staff member in charge of the field effort. The reason for this is that supervisors usually develop a close working relationship with interviewers and may find it more difficult to look objectively at possible infractions of the rules or indications of data fudging than a person who does not know the interviewers.

When the participants are contacted for the purpose of verifying the interview, factual questions that usually do not change in a short period of time, like the participant's number of years in school and current job status, are re-asked to make sure that the interview really took place. It is also a good opportunity to ask whether the interviewer was pleasant and arrived on time and whether the scheduled time was convenient for the participants. Interviewers may want to schedule interviews at times that coincide best with their own schedules (Alreck & Settle, 1985). This practice can be irritating to participants and may lead to unnecessary attrition in a subsequent assessment wave. A particularly relevant question to ask is whether the participant felt that the interview was conducted at the right pace. When interviewers are paid per completed interview, they may be inclined to rush through the interview and not give participants enough opportunity to think about their responses.

The verification process should also be used to check on errors or omissions that required the interviewer to re-contact the participant. This procedure will determine whether the answers given during the verification check differ from those reported by the interviewer or whether participants recall that the interviewer called back.

Positive feedback from the verification process should be relayed to the interviewers. Hearing about enthusiastic reactions from satisfied participants can be a morale booster. In addition, it tells the interviewers that verification of their interviews is taking place.

When fraud is suspected, additional checks may be necessary to establish a pattern of infractions. Checking of interviews may lead to the firing of an interviewer when fraud is discovered. Therefore, it is important that the verification process be standardized and carefully documented. In other words, when it is necessary to confront an interviewer, the evidence should be so clear and unequivocal that there can be no argument about the reason for dismissal. If an interviewer is fired, all of his or her previous work must be considered suspect and needs to be re-examined. Some of the interviews may have to be discarded and, if still possible, redone. Knowing that several verification procedures are in place will not only deter interviewers from fraud but also convince them of the value placed on correct information.

Monitoring Response Patterns

The interviewer's performance can also be examined by looking at the type of answers they have obtained for certain questions. This strategy applies especially to questions that require the interviewer to probe for multiple responses. One may suspect that high producers or interviewers who report relatively short interviewing times may discourage multiple responses or may not give respondents enough time to provide additional answers. Because of insufficient probing, these interviewers may also have a high percentage of "Don't Know" answers.

Error Rates

It is inevitable that errors are made in interviews. Although it may be possible to catch and correct errors, processing corrections is time-consuming for both the office staff and the interviewers. Most errors can be prevented by instructing interviewers to carefully edit interview schedules after an interview has been completed. If a high error rate still occurs, this may be evidence of general carelessness or inability of the interviewer to master the interview (Freeman & Butler, 1976).

When the data entry staff checks interview materials for completeness and correctness, they should create and maintain in the tracking system an error record for each interviewer so that individual rates of mistakes can be closely monitored. Interviewers should receive regular feedback on their error rates and, if necessary, suggestions should be made for improvement. If interviewers far exceed the average error rate repeatedly, they should be dismissed. On the other hand, improvements in error rates or very low error rates should not be overlooked and should be praised lavishly.

MORALE

When the data collection is in full swing and interviewers have settled into the routine of contacting and interviewing participants, supervisors should start thinking about ways to keep interviewers enthusiastic and interested in their work. There are several ways of keeping morale high. It goes without saying that continued support and frequent recognition of the interviewers' work by the office staff is important. Newsletters can communicate the progress of the study and include tips on handling specific situations, common errors, and better ways of dealing with certain questions. Newsletters can be particularly useful to convey information when interviewing takes place at multiple sites. Newsletters can also be used to announce which interviewer completed the most interviews or had the fewest errors. In addition, newsletters can communicate events like lectures and courses occurring in the institution, or birthdays, picnics, and parties occurring in the project.

To kindle the competitive spirit among the interviewers, contests may be held to reward the most productive interviewer of the week or the interviewer with the lowest error rate. Such competitions have a lasting effect on morale only if the staff makes a big deal out of the contests, if interviewers feel the prizes are worth competing for, and if the winners are announced with fanfare (Peters & Waterman, 1982).

CLOSING OUT THE ASSESSMENT WAVE

As the end of data collection nears and the pool of possible cases dwindles, the remaining participants are usually more difficult to find and harder to convince to do the interview. This group of final cases may be different from cases completed earlier in the study; it may include more individuals who frequently move around or who have two jobs and very little time to schedule an interview. A special effort should, therefore, be made to keep working on these cases to prevent any possibility of bias in the sample, and enough time should be allowed to complete them before data collection is discontinued. Supervisors will have to use all their skills to assist the interviewers in their final efforts and keep them motivated to go the extra mile. To simplify the task of supervising, it is a good strategy to consolidate the final cases in the hands of just a few interviewers. Each remaining interviewer will have a sufficient number of cases, thus making it attractive to continue working for the study. The time that supervisors usually spend on keeping track of a large pool of interviewers will be greatly reduced, and more hours can be devoted to difficult cases and hard-to-solve search problems.

Usually, attrition among interviewers at the end of the assessment phase occurs naturally. A small group of dedicated and effective interviewers remains with the project while the rest start looking for other employment. However, if supervisors have to select interviewers to close out the assessment wave, they should not use a high level of productivity as the only criterion for this decision. Supervisors should also consider interviewers who have low refusal rates, are tenacious, have excellent interpersonal and problem-solving skills, and have relatively few other commitments so that they have the flexibility to schedule interviews anytime. Also, interviewers who have a high success rate in turning around initially reluctant participants may be especially effective for the last part of the assessment phase.

Because obtaining the final interviews is so important, and because they usually require more time and energy to complete, a bonus system may be instituted that progressively adds more pay to each completed interview. Such a system is usually most effective when the interviewer pool has been narrowed down to one or two interviewers who will benefit considerably by completing those last cases.

INTERVIEWER DEBRIEFING

At the end of the data collection phase, there should be an opportunity to thank interviewers for their good work and to acknowledge that, without their special effort, the study would not be a success. If no other data collection phase is planned, this is also a good time to provide interviewers with additional information about the study and explain its objectives more extensively than was possible during training. Also, if some responses to questions in the interview were particularly upsetting to interviewers, these responses should be talked about in the debriefing session if they were not addressed already during supervision.

During the debriefing session, interviewers may be willing to tell the investigator what they liked and disliked about the assessment, which questions they felt were badly understood, and which parts of the interview were well received by the participants. Interviewers can provide researchers with valuable feedback about the interview schedule that they otherwise would not have known just by looking at the results of their analyses.

CONCLUSION

The work of the interviewers needs to be examined regularly. If their productivity is systematically evaluated, if their requests for assistance are followed up in a timely manner, and if the feedback they receive about the quality of their work is constructive, interviewers will feel that they are part of a well-managed operation that produces high quality work. A highly structured, computerized supervision system that can track the progress of the study on a day-to-day basis and answer questions concerning the workload of an individual interviewer or the status of a particular interview is pivotal. At all times the project staff needs to be able to obtain information about the status of the assessment phase, and this information needs to be made visible and monitored. When information concerning the progress of the study is readily available, researchers and supervisors will be able to make timely and targeted decisions when adjustments need to be made. The quality of the interviewers' work should be appraised by directly observing interviews in the field, listening to tape-recorded interviews, or obtaining feedback from interviews with phantom participants. A percentage of participants should also be called after the interview is completed to verify that the interview took place and to get the participant's perspective on the interviewer's work.

7

Data Management

The amount of time and money required for coding, checking, computerizing, and documenting the data is frequently underestimated in planning a study. Successful data management depends on a sound organization that has mapped out in advance all the data preparation, processing, and documentation steps and is ready to implement these steps when data collection is about to commence. In other words, the data management system should be fully operational *before* the project gets buried under an avalanche of incoming data that need to be coded, checked, and entered.

Data management needs to proceed on schedule because the timeliness of final products of a study depends on the availability of cleaned data files. Also, in studies with multiple assessment waves, the results from previous assessments may need to be examined to make adjustments in interview schedules or changes in interviewer training for the next assessment phase. Timely completion of the data management steps is mandatory when the sample selection for future assessments is based on the results of the current assessment.

In this chapter we consider the data management steps that are necessary to prepare data for statistical analyses. We discuss the data preparation and processing steps to produce clean data files. These include the tracking of materials, coding, computer-aided checking and data entry, and the handling of missing and conflicting information. Once the data files are clean, variables need to be created and a system needs to be set up to keep track of and document data transformations and newly created variables. We also discuss the need for archiving study materials, including data files, and suggest procedures for data sharing. Finally, we discuss the staff necessary for data management and software needs. Our data management approach applies specifically to studies that collect information with pencil and paper. When studies use scanning devices to computerize interview material or when interviewers type participants' answers directly into the computer some steps may not apply, but most of the data management steps that we outline will still need to be done.

DATA PREPARATION

When assessment materials come to the office for data entry, a number of procedures should be in place to ensure an efficient data entry process. These procedures include clear identification of all materials and the implementation of a data processing system that keeps track of every data management step.

Identification of Assessment Materials

Assessment materials often consist of more than one interview booklet, as may be the case when multiple informants in one household are interviewed. Interview materials may also involve loose sheets like consent forms, releases for information, and payment forms. Usually not all materials will stay together, and forms will be channeled to different people who take care of a variety of tasks related to the processing of the interview, such as payment of participants or filing of consent forms. *All* pages of assessment materials should be uniformly marked with an ID number so that they can always be linked to a participant when pages become detached. This task should be done by the interviewer at the completion of the assessment, using a number stamp that maximizes readability of ID numbers. To reduce the risk of accidental transposition of numbers, interviewers should first stamp the ID number on study material that contains the *printed* ID number, like the contact sheet. These two numbers can then be verified before stamping all other materials.

Identification of Assessment Phases

For studies with multiple assessment phases, all interview materials should have an assessment phase identifier. This is especially important when two or more assessment phases are going through data processing at the same time, creating a risk of entering data in the wrong file or filing materials in the wrong place. For easy identification, materials may be color coded to distinguish assessment phases or samples. Distinct colors can be used for the cover of interview schedules and for other materials like contact sheets, payment forms, and consent forms to make identification of materials from one assessment phase easy to distinguish from materials from another phase. It is best to avoid white, light grey, or cream colors because they are not obvious enough and can be mistaken for regular office materials like drafts of papers and thus accidentally end up in the wrong place.

Tracking of Data Preparation and Processing Steps

To make sure that all data preparation and processing steps are completed, all steps should be documented so that it is always possible to track which task was completed and who was responsible. One simple method of tracking is to require each data procedure to be dated and initialed on the cover page of the interview booklet. It is better, however, to keep track of the different data steps in a computer file. This procedure has the advantage that the steps can be traced without the need to look at the actual interview booklet, which is especially important when the material can be in many different places. For instance, assessment materials may pass from the interviewer to the supervisor, then to the data manager for coding and data entry, before being returned to the interviewer for corrections, and so on. In such an operation, there is ample opportunity for materials to be misplaced. If each data step can be traced in the computerized tracking file, it will be possible to track the last step completed in the processing of materials and to determine their most likely location.

DATA PROCESSING

The data processing includes coding, data checking, data entry, data entry verification, and data cleaning. The end product of the data processing steps are files of raw data in which errors and omissions have been corrected as much as possible and in which missing data are clearly labeled as to their source.

Coding

Before the data can be computerized, many structured interviews require some coding of open-ended responses. The reason for permitting open-ended responses may be that the content area is new for the investigator and it is not clear what the responses will be, or all the possible answers cannot be anticipated ahead of time. Another reason for allowing open-ended answers is that the coding of responses requires expert knowledge, as, for instance, in the case of responses related to prescription drugs.

The coding of open-ended questions and residual "other" categories should be one of the first steps in the data management process. Taking care of the coding immediately after the materials have been brought to the office allows coders to ask interviewers to obtain additional information if it is not possible to code the answer. In addition, if coding takes place before the data are entered, the necessity of including additional data steps to integrate the coded data into the data files is circumvented.

Early coding, however, requires that an exhaustive coding scheme be developed before the data are collected, which may not always be possible when there is uncertainly about the types of answers participants will give. As an alternative strategy, difficult-to-code responses to open-ended questions can be typed into the computer during data entry so that they can be reviewed when enough responses have been collected to make the development of a coding system possible.

Checking Assessment Materials for Completeness

Even with the best training and the most user-friendly instruments, interviewers will make errors. A high premium should be placed on keeping missing data to a minimum. Checking of assessment materials is often done by interviewer supervisors and involves visual scanning of the booklets. Visual checking can be cumbersome and prone to overlooking errors, especially when interview schedules contain many skipping patterns. As a consequence, additional mistakes may be discovered when the data are being entered into the computer. If much time has elapsed between the completion of assessments and data entry, it may not be possible or valid to recontact the participant to retrieve missing information.

To circumvent the problems with visual scanning of interview materials, data checking can be incorporated into the data entry procedure. To make this method of data checking effective, the computer program for data entry should be written in such a way that the visual display screens used for data entry closely resemble the pages in the interview schedule so that missed questions can be detected easily. For instance, if interviewers did not follow an instruction correctly and used the wrong skipping pattern, the to-be-entered fields shown on the computer screen will be different from the questions filled out in the interview schedule. The data entry programs should also check for out-of-range values and illogical answers. For instance, using amphetamines ten times without a doctor's prescription is inconsistent with an answer of five times overall use of this drug in the lead question.

Correcting Errors in Assessment Materials

Correcting errors should be the responsibility of the interviewer. To distinguish information that was obtained during the interview from corrections and information obtained from recontacting participants, interviewers should record all corrections and additional entries with a different color pen from that used when filling out the booklet initially. Supervisors should not assume automatically that problems with the interview materials are always resolved correctly. They should always check the corrections after the interviewers have dealt with them.

Not all errors require recontacting the participant. Sometimes the interviewer has not followed the correct recording method as specified in training or has forgotten to stamp the ID number on some of the pages in the interview schedule. Although it may be tempting for the supervisors or the data management team to make corrections for the interviewer, the tasks of the interviewer should be clearly separated from those of the supervisor and data management staff. It would be impossible to draw the line between which corrections can be made safely and where guesswork starts. Therefore, no compromises should be made, and interviewers should correct their own mistakes.

Data Entry Errors

Data entry programs that check for interviewer errors can also check for data entry errors like illogical entries and out-of-range values. In spite of these checks and the use of easy-to-follow data entry screens, keypunch errors are made and double entry verification is necessary. If data checking is incorporated into the first round of data entry, the second round of data entry can be used not only to verify the first entry but also to incorporate corrections made by interviewers in errors discovered during the first entry.

Alternative Methods of Data Entry

To reduce the amount of time spent on data entry and data verification, a scanning device may be a reasonable alternative for the computerization of data. Nowadays, special software can design interview forms that will allow the scanner to read answers recorded in designated spaces on a paper. Scanning devices can read numbers and bubble-filling fields with a high degree of accuracy, but the same cannot be said yet for the scanning of fields with alphanumeric information. Thus the scanned data of alphanumeric fields still have to be compared with the original information for possible discrepancies. Also, when scanning devices are used as an alternative to data entry, there is still a need to provide checks for missed questions, illogical answers, and out-of-range values.

When interviews are done by telephone or in an office, the information is frequently entered directly into computers. In addition, the advent of laptop or notebook computers has made it possible to use computers in field interviewing as well. Computer-aided interviewing avoids the cumbersome process of data entry and some data checking and data verification steps. It makes interviewing easier if the computer programs are written in such a way that they indicate which questions should be asked and which questions should be skipped, depending on earlier input. Computer-aided interviewing also can warn the interviewer for answers that are out of range or illogical. In field interviewing, the cost and upkeep of laptop computers is still a drawback and backup computers have to be available in case of an emergency. Another disadvantage of laptop computers is that field interviewers may not like to use expensive computers because of the increased likelihood of being robbed, or they may not be very handy when assessments have to be done outside in adverse weather conditions. Readers are referred to Saris (1991) for more information on computer-aided interviewing.

Identification of Missing Information

An effective data management team retrieves as much information as possible to complete missed questions and to clear up uncertainties in the participants' answers. Nonetheless, there are always errors that cannot be rectified, or there may be missing data because the participant did not know how to answer a question or the question did not apply to the participant. Information may also be missing because the participant refused to answer certain questions or no data were available because the participant was not interviewed in a particular assessment wave.

Missing data should be identified in such a way that the reason they are missing is clear from the coding scheme. For instance, it is important to know that a particular question has a large number of missing data because many participants did not understand the question. In a subsequent study or a follow-up assessment, the wording of the question may need to be adjusted, or the question may be eliminated from the interview schedule altogether. The reasons participants missed entire assessments is also important to keep track of because this information is used in the calculation of retention rates.

How to Deal With Duplicate and Discrepant Information

Even if all the questions have been answered, the information may be inconsistent or conflicting, and data management has to decide how to deal with this problem. Inconsistent information occurs when participants are asked basic information, like birthdays and Social Security numbers, at each assessment, or identical information is obtained from different sources, like a birth date supplied by the participant himself, by a caretaker, or by the school. Short of having access to official records like birth certificates or Social Security cards, there will never be absolute certainty which of the conflicting pieces of information was correct. When dealing with duplicate information, it may be necessary, for analysis purposes, to create a data file that, for each participant, contains a single data point with information that, after comparing all the available data, is considered most likely to be correct. To make this file as accurate as possible, participants can be recontacted to ask about discrepancies. This does not mean, however, that the conflicting data should be erased. Different and seemingly incorrect birthdays may be valuable. A birth date of a participant provided by a school may not match the date that was supplied by the mother but may match the birth date on court records. Relying exclusively on the birth date obtained from the mother could lead to the wrong assumption that court records carrying the same name as the participant but having a different birth date do not belong to the participant. Thus, for identification purposes, optimal matching is best accomplished by maintaining and using as much information as possible, even if some of that information is incorrect.

Data Protection

Identifiable information like names and addresses should be removed from the interview schedule and stored in a locked place. In longitudinal studies such information can be kept in participants' personal files, together with contact and payment sheets and correspondence. Access to this information can be safeguarded more easily when the identifiable information from all assessment phases is kept together. Personal files that store information from different phases also provide easy searching for previous addresses, the names of former husbands, and the telephone numbers of relatives who may know the participant's whereabouts. For computerized information that requires special protection, computer programs can limit access to data files or identifiable information in data files can be scrambled.

DATA MANAGEMENT STAFF

The data manager is the person who is responsible for making sure that the incoming information is coded, computerized, and documented in such a way that the data are accessible for analysis purposes. If the project is large, one of the data manager's main functions is the *supervision* of coding, data entry, and data cleaning staff. This includes assigning members of the data management team to the appropriate tasks and making sure that these tasks are completed in a timely fashion. The data manager should also be responsible for keeping analysis documentation current and preparing data sets for in-house and outside analysts. Data managers should have good programming skills and be familiar with all the computer hardware and software used in the project. If the computer programming jobs are large and recurrent, a separate individual may have to be hired to assist in programming tasks.

Supervision of Data Management Staff

The same principles that guide the supervision of interviewers can be used in data management by making the progress of the different data management steps and the production of individual staff members as visible as possible. This goal can be accomplished by requiring weekly reports on the progress of the different data management components and by keeping track of the performance of each member of the data management team. This is particularly important when data management staff work part-time or irregular hours, as is often the case when students are used.

Quality Control

Coding, data checking, and data entry require attention to detail. These jobs, however, are monotonous and, in themselves, not very rewarding. The data manager should make every effort to impress on the data entry and coding staff how important it is that their jobs are executed well. Like interviewers, the data processing staff should be thoroughly trained and have manuals with instructions on how the assessment materials need to be filled out and what kinds of errors to watch out for. During and after training, *practice* interviews should be coded and entered from time to time to ensure that all coders and data entry persons are doing their jobs well and catch tricky errors.

How to Keep Up With the Field Effort

If coding, checking, and data entry are done in tandem with data collection, materials need to be processed quickly so that booklets with errors can be given back to interviewers and corrections can be taken care of in a timely manner. In the beginning of an assessment period, the volume of interviews is usually much higher than later on. For example, in an assessment phase scheduled to last about 5 months, it is not unlikely that about 70% of the interviews are completed in the first 2 months and 90% in the first 3 months, with the remaining 10% requiring an additional 2 months for completion. Given this scenario, it may be unavoidable that some staff need to be laid off or given other tasks when data collection is slowing down. Another option is to hire a smaller data management staff and expect them to work additional hours in the beginning of an assessment phase. In this way one avoids spending time and money on the hiring and training of people who are only briefly needed.

DATA DOCUMENTATION

An important function of the data management team is the documentation of data files. Data files need to be preserved in an organized fashion. Computer resource limitations usually prevent projects with extensive assessments or studies with multiple data collection phases from storing all the data in a single data file. In addition, different types of data require setting up files with different kinds of file structures. For example, unique information like date of birth, socioeconomic status, and ethnic background most likely will have one record per participant. On the other hand, files that store information on family members or life events may need a separate record for each family member or each reported event. Also, in longitudinal studies, it may be more economical to maintain separate data files for each assessment wave. Not every instrument may be used in all assessment waves, and not all participants may agree to be interviewed at every assessment period. If all the information for multiple assessment waves were to be stored in one file, there would be many empty data cells. Thus each research project usually has to maintain a collection of different data files that will be part of a *data bank* that can be accessed for future data analysis. Keeping all information up to date in a data bank with multiple files is a complicated task and requires a catalog of files that details the content of each file, how the file was created, and when the file was last updated.

Each study will need a system to organize its files. In our project we distinguish between *three sets of files*.

The first type of file contains the assessment data in a cleaned and coded format. The data in these files are called raw variables and are the result of the data management steps discussed above.

The second type of file contains derived variables. In many instances, raw data are not used in analyses in their original format but are transformed or combined with other raw variables to create derived variables. For instance, responses to individual questions from a single measurement instrument may be added to form a summary score. A derived variable can also involve just a single raw variable that is recoded, as is the case when a continuous variable is dichotomized. Normalized variables or data for which missing values have been imputed are also included in this category.

The third type of file contains information related to the data collection effort such as files that keep track of the participant's address, payments, and consent status. The importance of these files in monitoring the interviewer's performance and the tracking of the field effort have been discussed in Chapter 6.

Naming of Raw Variables

Each study needs to develop a system of naming raw variables. We use a system that makes variable names unique and easy to trace within each data phase and across data phases. Our assessment schedule consists of a compilation of many instruments developed by various research groups, with the questions numbered within each instrument. We did not attempt to renumber all the questions of the interview schedule in consecutive order so that each question had a unique number but rather gave each instrument an instrument number and preserved the original numbering within the instruments. The name for each variable starts with the phase identifier followed by the number for the instrument and the number of the question. For each assessment wave, data books are created that contain the instruments and printouts of the frequencies of all variables. Coded variables or variables with additional codes that are not included in the instrument are provided with value labels that explain the meaning of the answer categories. The names of the files that store raw variables can be recognized by the phase identifier and the instrument number.

Naming and Keeping Track of Derived Variables

For smaller projects it may be possible to identify derived variables in such a way that the name of each variable reflects the content of the data field. Although this procedure may eliminate an explanation of the variable names and make analysis printouts easy to examine, it will be hard to prevent the duplication of variable names when the study starts to expand and when variables are created by different people. Thus the naming of derived variables should also be done systematically and may include the initial of the person who created the variable and an identifier for the phase(s) from which the raw data originated.

Many of the derived variables will simply be total scale scores for an assessment instrument. Computing these variables can take place at a set time, such as at the end of data cleaning. If the creation of these derived variables is integrated into data management as a routine procedure, it will be relatively easy to maintain a catalog of these variables with documentation that includes all arithmetic transformations, recoding procedures, value labeling statements, and routine procedures like internal reliability testing.

Derived variables that are constructed during the data analysis process are much harder to track. Documentation for these variables may be embedded in files with statistical analysis procedures, or worse, may not exist at all if they were created interactively without the existence of a log documenting the algorithms. These kinds of derived variables are often part of temporary data files and are not permanently saved unless a special effort is made to transfer them to a separate file.

The only way to keep track of derived variables constructed in the analysis process and to have the ability to reconstruct them is to request that, for each new derived variable, the analysis staff provides data management with procedural files that contain data transformation algorithms and the variables resulting from these transformations.

To keep track of derived variables, we have set up a data bank that is able to retrieve the following information about each variable: (a) description of the content, (b) the raw variables included in creating the derived variable, (c) the construction date, (d) the name of the procedural file that created the variable, (e) the person responsible for constructing the derived variable, and (f) the publication(s) in which the variable was used. This system facilitates the reconstruction of previously reported results. It enables any user of the data set to search for existing derived variables and avoids duplication of effort or the creation of slightly different variables intended to cover similar characteristics or behaviors.

When errors are discovered in raw variables, as inevitably will happen at times, the system permits the identification of all derived variables in which these flawed raw variables were included. The system also enables tracking of publications in which the derived variables were used. Thus the impact of the problem can be quickly assessed and adjustments can be made (Freedland & Carney, 1992). Information about data errors also needs to be broadcast to analysts working on project data that have not yet been logged into the system. Thus it is important to keep track not only of variables that have been used in the past but also of variables that are in circulation at the time an error was discovered.

Archiving Project Materials

Buildings can go up in flames, burglars may walk off with computers containing hard drives packed with information, and hard drives do crash at times. To prevent these events from being disastrous, materials need to be archived in a place away from the office. Archiving study materials means more than regularly backing up data files and maintaining copies of data files in a place away from the study office. The researcher has to consider other materials like instruments, training manuals, coding books, data tracking and data entry programs, files that keep track of participants and contain their names and addresses, and files that are used to generate derived variables and statistical analyses. A distinction should be made between materials that do not change and have to be archived only once and materials that have to be updated from time to time. In this way, periodic updating only involves additional project materials and updated data files. It is easy to archive materials on diskettes, removable hard drives, magnetic tape, or mainframe computers; the trick is to do it regularly by having fixed dates for this task.

DATA SHARING

Sharing data with researchers outside of the immediate project staff can be a tremendous benefit to a project. Other researchers may have different points of view from the original research team or a different expertise that may broaden and increase the yield from a study. In addition, the original findings of a research team may be verified, refined, or even contradicted by outside researchers (Kielcolt & Nathan, 1985).

Projects with large data sets are usually bombarded by outside requests to have access to the data set. Even though the research team may be enthusiastic about a proposal for analysis, they may not have the proper means to deal with the work that accompanies such requests. Data preparation can be time-consuming and, even with the best documentation available, the research staff will still have to respond to questions by outside users concerning issues or conventions that are clear for the research group but not for outside users. This data sharing may be even more of a burden for the investigator when the project has been completed and most of the staff has been terminated.

If necessary, the project should be prepared to request reimbursement for the preparation of data sets and for providing assistance at a later date. Investigators will generally only very reluctantly come to the conclusion that they must charge for the privilege of using their data set. However, when the burden of servicing outside projects becomes detrimental to the ongoing work of the research group, requesting a contribution becomes a necessity. Funding agencies have generally not set aside funds to deal with outside users, although many agencies specifically demand that data sets be moved into the public domain at the completion of a project. Requiring some remuneration for services has the added advantage of deterring individuals who are not strongly committed to using the data.

Data sharing with outside researchers requires a clear understanding of how the data will be used and for what purpose. To prevent any unpleasantness, a data sharing contract should be drawn up to specify who will have access to which part of a data set and for how long. The contract should include an outline of the questions to be addressed and an analysis plan to make sure that the data are not misinterpreted or later used for a different purpose. The outline also serves to "claim" an area of research so that others know that someone is using the data for that purpose. The investigator may preserve the right to examine the results before they are disseminated, not to act as a censor but to ensure that the data have been interpreted correctly and that there is no unnecessary duplication in reporting. Such a contract should also specify the kind of help that the original research group will provide. In general, outside users are advised not to work in isolation on a "borrowed" data set, but to work closely with the original research group. When the premises for collaboration have been clearly specified, working together on a data set benefits all parties.

SELECTING COMPUTER SOFTWARE

Most likely more than one computer software package has to be used to take care of all data management, analyses, and report writing tasks of a study. Because a good data management system is the key to both the speedy completion of the data collection and the efficient processing of the data, we will discuss the choice of this system first and then discuss the need for other software to cover additional project demands.

We do not know of ready-to-use computerized data management systems that will keep track of all the data collection and data processing steps that we have mentioned. Some progress has been made in the marketing of computer-assisted telephone interviewing software that includes management systems that can generate telephone numbers for interviewers, keep track of the outcome of calls, and determine when to call next. Such systems can also produce day-to-day status reports, change priorities of telephone numbers when necessary, and assign telephone numbers to specific interviewers (for an overview of such systems, see Saris, 1991).

For most projects that involve keeping track of data collected with pencil-and-paper interviews, researchers will have to develop their own system using data management software not specifically developed for that purpose. Fortunately, the majority of the data management systems currently on the market are perfectly adequate to handle such a task. Although the choice of one system over another is usually influenced by familiarity with a particular software package or by advice from colleagues, it is important to consider how widely the system is currently used, how easy the system is to use, and whether the system interfaces with other software packages.

The choice of a data management system does not have to be guided by which system has the most powerful query capabilities or the fanciest menus to help users master data manipulation tasks. Rather, one is advised to look for software that is supported by the institution sponsoring the project so that technical backup is readily available. It can be costly and time-consuming to read user manuals or phone the software company's support services to figure out how to use a package. If a particular package is widely used in the institution where the research takes place, others can be consulted when problems occur and ideas can be traded with them. The availability of publications in local bookstores with easy-to-follow instructions, program ideas, and examples of how to deal with certain problems is another factor that may influence the choice of a data management package.

A user-friendly data management package is very important if the goal is to make most staff members "data management" literate. This criterion may eliminate from consideration complex systems that offer great flexibility and a wide range of possibilities but require very specialized skills to operate. It is a great advantage if staff members with only a rudimentary knowledge of computers can master uncomplicated data management tasks such as creating a file or looking up a participant's record. If the sponsoring institution offers introductory courses in the use of a particular data management software package, this may be a another factor in the selection of a data management package.

Additional Software Needs

Adding software is advisable only when absolutely necessary. For instance, the data management software that one is favoring may not be designed to keep track of the budget as elegantly as computer software specifically written for bookkeeping purposes; however, it may be perfectly adequate and not warrant the burden of having to deal with additional software.

Most data management software packages are capable of performing some descriptive statistics and producing simple graphs, but hardly ever do they satisfy all the project's needs for analyses and report writing. In this case, adding other software packages cannot be circumvented, and the researcher needs to know whether a data management system has a direct interface with the additional software so that files can easily be imported and exported between the different systems. A good interface system should include not only the interchange of data but also the interchange of data types and variable names.

Some statistical packages currently on the market have data management capabilities, are able to set up databases and use programs to facilitate data entry and other management tasks, and produce publication-ready figures and graphs. Thus, for some research projects with uncomplicated housekeeping needs, it is a good approach to first evaluate whether a statistical package will serve the project's data management requirements before investing in separate software.

CONCLUSION

The survival of a longitudinal study depends to a large extent on the ability to produce results in a timely fashion. Structuring how the information resulting from the interviews will be processed, made available for data analysis, documented, and stored is central to good data management. Care needs to be bestowed on the data from the time of arrival in the office to the final publications. Rigorous data management requires preparation and resources, as well as a system that is able to keep track of data sets. Data sets in the system should include files with variables in their original format as well data sets with derived variables that were created in preparation for analyses. Keeping track of derived variables and the way they were constructed makes it possible to reconstruct previous results when requested. Measures of quality control need to be implemented at all levels. In complicated data sets, some problems that were overlooked or could not have been foreseen during data verification and cleaning become apparent only when the data are being analyzed. It is, therefore, essential that analysis staff, when preparing for statistical analyses, carefully scrutinize frequencies and other simple statistics like contingency tables to make sure that the data are correct and internally consistent.

8

Quality Control and Research Ethics

In Chapter 1 we mentioned three general tasks involved in the management of projects: the management of staff, cost containment, and quality control. These three tasks require extensive planning before a project begins so that most of the logistics and budgetary matters are worked out. However, it should be clear that planning and keeping an eye on the time-line and budget are tasks that *continue* throughout the life of the project and that concern *all* members of the team, not only the investigator. Everybody should feel responsible for implementing and monitoring the time-lines, everybody should feel responsible for keeping the budget under control, and everybody should keep the quality of data and the resulting study products uppermost in their minds.

Management of staff, cost containment, and quality control are not mutually exclusive or unrelated activities. If staff are badly supervised, money is wasted and the quality of the data is negatively affected. If the budget runs out before its time, staff may have to be laid off, and certain tasks will not be accomplished. If there are too many compromises in the quality of the data, the study might just as well not have been done and *all* money has been wasted.

QUALITY CONTROL

The quality of the data can be seen as the *keystone* of a project's success, and perfection should be the standard to strive for on all levels of the operation. Whenever there is a choice to be made between a strategy that would result in better, more complete data and one that is easier or less expensive, one should automatically lean to what makes the study more perfect. Of course budgetary constraints need to be taken into account, but decisions that reduce quality should not be taken lightly, and alternatives should be thoroughly explored. Inevitably, there will be circumstances that one had not foreseen that will make a study less than perfect; one should not consciously add to these. In a large study there are *daily temptations* to make decisions that slide the study a tiny notch away from the ideal. Each decision alone does not seem to be an important concession. Over time, however, many such unimportant decisions may compromise the study.

The attitude of striving for the best should be set from the top. Once such a climate has been set, staff know what is expected and may go to extraordinary lengths to do the best possible job. High standards are maintained only if project leaders recognize exceptional performance in terms of creative problem solving, persistence, or just sheer amount of work. It is, therefore, important that persistence in searching for participants or creativity in solving scheduling problems be publicly applauded. In the same vein, interviewers who have low error and refusal rates should be acknowledged. Seemingly small things, like a well-organized supervisor's office, a neatly laid-out form, or careful notes of meetings should be encouraged.

Concern for quality does not stop at the interviewers' level. Data cleaning, data analyses, and data documentation should be subject to the same scrutiny and the same standards. The goal is to ensure that the product of the study is not flawed because of sloppy decisions, carelessness, or errors that could have been prevented. A secondary goal is to be able to reconstruct what has happened to the data and to make it possible for others to use the data with the help of documentation. These are not trivial or easy-to-reach goals. Shapiro and Charrow (1989) have reported shortcomings in data management (quality control, documentation, and archiving) in more than 20% of routine data audits done on research conducted for the Food and Drug Administration in the United States. Other researchers have also noted an alarming number of instances of data mismanagement (Prud'homme, Canner, & Cutler, 1989; van der Putten, van der Velden, Siers, & Hamersma, 1987). These lapses do not refer to intentional deception or fraud in scientific research but to unintentional errors and carelessness in, or lack of the documentation of, data collection, data management, or analyses.

The term "audit worthiness" has been coined to stand for good housekeeping in data management and analysis (Freedland & Carney, 1992). The larger the data set and the larger the number of researchers who are working on it, the more difficult it is to impose accountability and to set uniform standards for data and analysis management, but the more necessary such standards become. Anyone who has ever indulged in a quick, weakly documented burst of data analysis, and who after a month had difficulty in reconstructing the analysis process, knows how easy it is to fall for the temptation to just go ahead and not document and how difficult it is to make sense of one's work afterward.

Schwandt and Halpern (1988) have suggested that even if one does not expect a formal outside evaluation, one needs to form an audit trail that would allow an independent evaluator to assess procedures, decisions, and conclusions from the results. The term "audit" should not strike terror into the heart of the investigator or any of the staff, but should be considered as a yardstick by which to measure the adequacy of the documentation.

RESEARCH ETHICS

Quality control should not be implemented just because it safeguards against mistakes that would be embarrassing to report to the research community or the funding agency. It should be important for the researcher and the rest of the team to know that the research has intellectual integrity and that the results are to be trusted. Quality control is an issue of research ethics.

The effects of sloppy research can be as bad as those of outright fraud. Regardless of the intent, both deliver incorrect results, and the researcher can be held responsible for the quality of the data in either case. Sometimes, the border between sloppiness and fraud is hazy. For instance, when, in reporting participation rates, no-contact households are left out, thereby increasing the participation rate, is that fraud, unethical reporting, or an oversight? Circumstances, such as a mother being drunk during the interview, may be known to the supervisor but somehow not reported to the data management staff. The reason may be that the supervisor forgot about it, or that he or she did not want to be bothered with the consequences of acknowledging that the interview was invalid; that is, reprimanding the interviewer for conducting an interview under such circumstances and having the interview redone. Thus there are many relatively *passive* ways in which the results can become close to fraudulent.

Kimmel (1988) summarized the ways in which data can be *actively* manipulated. *Cooking* consists of the selection of only those data that fit the hypothesis. *Trimming* is the manipulation of data to make them look better. *Forging* is the fabrication of data. Trimming and forging may occur not only at the level of data analysis and report writing but also at the data collection or data managing stage.

Earlier we discussed ways to avoid compromises in quality of data collection by having an extensive system of quality control, which makes it almost certain that forgers will be caught. Such a system works preventively in that interviewers know they will lose their jobs if they succumb to the temptation to forge. Another way to prevent fraud is to have more than one person work on a crucial task. If two supervisors are using the same database to track interviewer progress, it will be difficult for one supervisor to perform some sleight of hand. Similarly, if analyses for a publication are shared by two analysts, the chances of analysis errors or a misinterpretation of the data may be lessened. Also, if products of a study are discussed by the whole staff, it is more difficult to introduce interpretations of the data that are not quite supported by the findings.

Honest errors or omissions may occur, however, and it is important that they do not become an occasion for trimming or forging, as may happen if the cost of admitting errors or omissions is high. Admitting shortcomings should be an occasion for brainstorming rather than for denigration or punishment. In this way, the necessity of hiding the actual performance by fraud is taken away and better ways of reaching the goals can be developed. On the other hand, researchers should not hesitate to fire staff members who compromise the research effort.

In case one's conscience does not put up sufficiently strong barriers against sloppy or fraudulent research, the realization of the potentially devastating consequences to the researcher should be ample warning. These consequences range from having one's work always treated with suspicion, being barred from research funds, and losing one's position, to imprisonment.

Relationship With Participants

Ethical standards also govern the research team's relationship with research participants. Most research requires consent forms, which are *legal documents* and should be treated as such. Participation is voluntary and can occur only after the potential participant has been informed about the study. Researchers should make sure that properly executed and signed consent forms (i.e., signed and initialed in all places and by the right person) are always on file. Thus audit worthiness should also apply to consent forms.

Generally, one of the conditions mentioned in the consent forms is that the information obtained from participants will be kept confidential. To maintain confidentiality, assessment materials containing identifiers should be kept in locked files or rooms. Although materials may *end up* in locked filing cabinets or locked rooms, there may be an interim in which the condition of confidentiality is not quite met. The materials may be lying around in the supervisor's office, the data entry office, or any other temporary place. Under such circumstances, interview booklets could be perused by anyone, including the cleaning staff. Constant vigilance is required to keep all materials, including address lists, names of relatives, and payment files, confidential *at all times.*

Concern about confidentiality is also shown in making sure that all staff understand the issue of confidentiality and in enforcing the standard that no one on the staff talk idly about participants, even without using names.

Issues of confidentiality can also arise when data are shared. Even though no identifying information is shared, participants may be recognizable from the files because they are the only murderer of a certain age in a certain year in a city or the only person from a class who became a surgeon.

Concerns may also arise if a study identifies an area by name or by ethnic group and reports findings that could reflect negatively on the area or group (Sieber, 1992). In reporting results, one should be sensitive to the feelings of others and not unnecessarily expose people to negative consequences.

Breaches in ethics with regard to the project's relationship with its participants can lead to investigations by Institutional Review Boards or funding agencies, which may stop a study or jeopardize future studies.

CONCLUSION

It should be clear from the contents of this book that conducting a high quality and ethical study is every staff member's business. It is not only the project manager who needs to be concerned about timeliness, budget, quality, and ethical issues; it is also the interviewers, secretary, statistician, file clerk, and, most of all, the principal investigators.

Investigators cannot hide behind ignorance. They are ultimately responsible for the conduct of the research team and should be informed about decisions and procedures on a regular basis. Conducting a research study is not something that only the "hired hands" do, while the investigator is isolated from the daily practical concerns to write papers.

Being aware of how the research is actually done is necessary because the investigator is responsible not only for the conduct of the study but also for the interpretation of the results. Investigators and, for that matter, all staff members who analyze data and write reports can benefit from attending the training of interviewers and coders and from accompanying interviewers in the field. They will gain a better understanding of what the numbers in the files really represent, and they will be confronted with the strengths, weaknesses, and peculiarities of the data collection and management procedures. This active involvement will help them in analysis decisions and the interpretation of the results. It will also help in creating understanding for the work of one's colleagues.

Problems encountered by one team member are the concern of the whole group, and it should be the responsibility of all team members to suggest new solutions for thorny problems or to help develop more efficient or more user-friendly procedures. In order to accomplish this goal, we schedule a brainstorming session for the whole staff twice a year with just this purpose in mind: to get other members of the team to think about problems with which their colleagues are struggling. Thus no section of the staff can work completely independently from, and in ignorance of, the work of other staff members. There has to be a team spirit and a team concern for other staff members' work. It is the role of the investigators and project managers not only to set high expectations and give directions but also to give team members the confidence that, together, they can do an outstanding job.

References

Alreck, P. L., & Settle, R. B. (1985). *The survey research handbook.* Homewood, IL: Richard D. Irwin.

American Statistical Association Conference. (1974). Report on the ASA Conference on Surveys of Human Populations. *The American Statistician, 28,* 30-34.

Anderson, B. A., Silver, B. D., & Abramson, P. R. (1988). The effects of race of the interviewer on measures of electoral participation by blacks in SRC national election studies. *Public Opinion Quarterly, 52,* 53-83.

Bailar, B. A. (1989). Issues in the design of panel surveys. In D. Kasprzyk, G. Duncan, G. Kalton, & M. P. Singh (Eds.), *Panel surveys* (pp. 1-24). New York: John Wiley.

Ball, J. C., & Brown, B. S. (1977). Institutional sources of data. In L. D. Johnston, D. N. Nurco, & L. N. Robins (Eds.), *Conducting follow-up research on drug treatment programs* (pp. 98-104). Washington, DC: Government Printing Office.

Billiet, J., & Loosveldt, G. (1988). Improvement of the quality of responses to factual survey questions by interviewer training. *Public Opinion Quarterly, 52,* 190-221.

Capaldi, D., & Patterson, G. R. (1987). An approach to the problem of recruitment and retention rates for longitudinal research. *Behavioral Assessment, 9,* 169-177.

Cleary, P., Mechanic, D., & Weiss, N. (1981). The effect of interviewer characteristics on responses to a mental health interview. *Journal of Health and Social Behavior, 22,* 183-193.

Cohen, J. (1977). *Statistical power analysis for the behavioral sciences* (Rev. ed.). Orlando, FL: Academic Press.

Copeland, A. P., & White, K. M. (1991). *Studying families.* Newbury Park, CA: Sage.

Cordray, S., & Polk, K. (1983). The implications of respondent loss in panel studies of deviant behavior. *Journal of Research in Crime and Delinquency, 20,* 214-242.

Davies, J. B., & Baker, R. (1987). The impact of self-presentation and interviewer bias effects on self-reported heroin use. *British Journal of Addiction, 82,* 907-912.

Davis, J. A., & Smith, T. W. (1992). *The NORC general social survey.* Newbury Park, CA: Sage.

Denzin, N. K. (1989). *Interpretive interactionism.* Newbury Park, CA: Sage.

Dijkstra, W. (1987). Interviewing style and respondent behavior: An experimental study of survey-interview. *Sociological Methods and Research, 16,* 309-334.

Farrington D. P., Gallagher, B., Morley, L., St. Ledger, R., & West, D. J. (1990). Minimizing attrition in longitudinal research: Methods of tracing and securing cooperation in a 24-year follow-up study. In D. Magnusson & L. R. Bergman (Eds.), *Data quality in longitudinal research* (pp. 122-147). Cambridge, UK: Cambridge University Press.

Fowler, F. J., Jr., & Mangione, T. W. (1990). *Standardized survey interviewing: Minimizing interviewer-related error.* Newbury Park, CA: Sage.

Freedland, K. E., & Carney, R. M. (1992). Data management and accountability in behavioral and biomedical research. *American Psychologist, 47,* 640-645.

Freeman, J., & Butler, E. W. (1976). Some sources of interviewer variance in surveys. *Public Opinion Quarterly, 40,* 79-91.

Frey, J. H. (1983). *Survey research by telephone.* Beverly Hills, CA: Sage.

Groves, R. M. (1989). *Survey errors and survey costs.* New York: John Wiley.

Groves, R. M., Cialdini, R. B., & Couper, M. P. (1992). Understanding the decision to participate in a survey. *Public Opinion Quarterly, 56,* 475-495.

Groves, R. M., & Fultz, N. H. (1985). Gender effects among telephone interviewers in a survey of economic attitudes. *Sociological Methods and Research, 14,* 31-52.

Groves, R. M., & Kahn, R. L. (1979). *Surveys by telephone: A national comparison with personal interviews.* New York: Academic Press.

Hedrick, T. E., Bickman, L., & Rog, D. J. (1993). *Applied research design: A practical guide.* Newbury Park, CA: Sage.

Henry, G. T. (1990). *Practical sampling.* Newbury Park, CA: Sage.

Hochstim, J. R. (1967). A critical comparison of three strategies of collecting data from households, *American Statistical Association Journal, 62,* 976-989.

Hornik, J. (1987). The effect of touch and gaze upon compliance and interest of interviewees. *Journal of Social Psychology, 127,* 681-683.

Huizinga, D., Loeber, R., & Thornberry, T. P. (1993). *Urban delinquency and substance use: Technical report.* Washington, DC: Office of Juvenile Justice and Delinquency Prevention, U.S. Department of Justice.

Jessor, R., & Jessor, S. L. (1977). *Problem behavior and psychosocial development: A longitudinal study of youth.* New York: Academic Press.

Jorgensen, D. L. (1989). *Participant observation.* Newbury Park, CA: Sage.

Kalton, G. (1983). *Introduction to survey sampling.* Beverly Hills, CA: Sage.

Kane, E. W., & Macaulay, L. J. (1993). Interviewer gender and gender attitudes. *Public Opinion Quarterly, 57,* 1-28.

Karweit, N., & Meyers, D. (1983). Computers in survey research. In P. H. Rossi, J. D. Wright, & A. B. Anderson (Eds.), *Handbook of survey research* (pp. 379-414). New York: Academic Press.

Kasprzyk, D., Duncan, G., Kalton, G., & Singh, M. P. (Eds.). (1989). *Panel surveys.* New York: John Wiley.

Kielcolt, K. J., & Nathan, L. E. (1985). *Secondary analysis of survey data.* Newbury Park, CA: Sage.

Kimmel, A. J. (1988). *Ethics and values in applied social research.* Newbury Park, CA: Sage.

Kish, L. (1965). *Survey sampling.* New York: Wiley.

Kraemer, C. H., & Thiemann, S. (1987). *How many subjects? Statistical power analysis in research.* Newbury Park, CA: Sage.

Lavrakas, P. (1993). *Telephone survey methods.* Newbury Park, CA: Sage.

Lipsey, M. W. (1990). *Design sensitivity: Statistical power for experimental research.* Newbury Park, CA: Sage.

Little, R. J. A., & Rubin, D. B. (1989). The analysis of social science data with missing values. *Sociological Methods and Research, 18,* 292-326.

Mangione, T. W. (1995). *Mail surveys: Improving the quality.* Thousand Oaks, CA: Sage.

Marin, G., & Marin, B. V. (1991). *Research with Hispanic populations.* Newbury Park, CA: Sage.

Marshall, C., & Rossman, B. (1989). *Designing qualitative research.* Newbury Park, CA: Sage.

Maruyama, G., & Deno, S. (1992). *Research in educational settings*. Newbury Park, CA: Sage.

Menard, S. (1991). *Longitudinal research*. Newbury Park, CA: Sage.

Miller, D. C. (1991). *Handbook of research design and social measurement* (5th ed.). Newbury Park, CA: Sage.

Nurco, D. N., Robins, L. N., & O'Donnell, J. A. (1977). Locating respondents. In L. D. Johnston, D. N. Nurco, & L. N. Robins (Eds.), *Conducting follow up research on drug treatment programs* (pp. 71-84). Washington, DC: Government Printing Office.

Oksenberg, L., Coleman, L., & Cannell, C. F. (1986). Interviewers' voices and refusal rates in telephone surveys. *Public Opinion Quarterly, 50*, 97-111.

Peters, T. J., & Waterman, R. H., Jr. (1982). *In search of excellence*. New York: Harper & Row.

Prewitt, K. (1983). Management of survey organizations. In P. H. Rossi, J. D. Wright, & A. B. Anderson (Eds.), *Handbook of survey research* (pp. 123-144). New York: Academic Press.

Prud'homme, G. J., Canner, P. L., & Cutler, J. A. (1989). Quality assurance and monitoring in the Hypertension Prevention Trial. *Controlled Clinical Trials, 10*(Suppl.), 84S-94S.

Robins, L. N. (1976). Problems in follow-up studies. *American Journal of Psychiatry, 134*, 904-907.

Robles, N., Flaherty, D. G., & Day, N. L. (1994). Retention of resistant subjects in longitudinal studies: Description and procedures. *American Journal of Drug and Alcohol Abuse, 20*, 87-100.

Rossi, P. H., Wright, J. D., & Anderson, A. B. (Eds.). (1983). *Handbook of survey research*. New York: Academic Press.

Saris, W. E. (1991). *Computer-assisted interviewing*. Newbury Park, CA: Sage.

Schwandt, T. A., & Halpern, E. S. (1988). *Linking auditing and meta evaluation*. Newbury Park, CA: Sage.

Shapiro, M. F., & Charrow, R. P. (1989). The role of data audits in detecting scientific misconduct: Results of the FDA program. *Journal of the American Medical Association, 262*, 2505-2511.

Sieber, J. (Ed.). (1991). *Sharing social science data. Advantages and challenges*. Newbury Park, CA: Sage.

Sieber, J. (1992). *Planning ethnically responsible research*. Newbury Park, CA: Sage.

Singer, E., Frankel, M. R., & Glassmann, M. B. (1983). The effect of interviewer characteristics and expectations on response. *Public Opinion Quarterly, 47*, 68-83.

Singer, E. M. (1978). The effect on informed consent procedures on respondents' reactions to surveys. *Journal for Market Research, 5*, 49-57.

Steeh, C. S. (1981). Trends in non-response rates, 1952-1979. *Public Opinion Quarterly, 45*, 40-57.

Stouthamer-Loeber, M., van Kammen, W., Loeber, R., Miller, D., & Kumer, B. (1992). *Contacting and interviewing subjects: Report #2*. Prepared for the Program on Human Development and Criminal Behavior, Harvard School of Public Health, Beslon, MA.

Sudman, S., & Kalton, G. (1986). New developments in the sampling of special populations. *Annual Review of Sociology, 12*, 401-429.

Swires-Hennessy, E., & Drake, M. (1992). The optimum time at which to conduct survey interviews [Special Issue: Market research in government decision making]. *Journal of the Market Research Society, 34*, 61-72.

Thomas, R. D. (1990). *How to investigate by computer*. Austin, TX: Thomas Publications.

Tuckel, P. S., & Feinberg, B. M. (1991). The answering machine poses many questions for telephone survey researchers. *Public Opinion Quarterly, 55*, 200-217.

Turnbull, J. E., McLeod, J. D., Callahan, J. M., & Kessler, R. C. (1988). Who should ask? Ethical interviewing in psychiatric epidemiology studies. *American Journal of Orthopsychiatry, 58*, 228-239.

van der Putten, E., van der Velden, J. W., Siers, A., & Hamersma, E. A. M. (1987). A pilot study on the quality of data management in a cancer clinical trial. *Controlled Clinical Trials, 8*, 96-100.

Vigderhous, G. (1981). Scheduling telephone interviews: A study of seasonal patterns. *Public Opinion Quarterly, 45*, 250-259.

Weinberg, E. (1983). Data collection: Planning and management. In P. H. Rossi, J. D. Wright, & A. B. Anderson (Eds.), *Handbook of survey research* (pp. 329-358). New York: Academic Press.

Weiss, C. H. (1968). Validity of welfare mothers' interview responses. *Public Opinion Quarterly, 32*, 622-633.

Weller, S. C., & Romney, A. K. (1988). *Systematic data collection.* Newbury Park, CA: Sage.

Yin, R. K. (1994). *Applications of case study research.* Newbury Park, CA: Sage.

Author Index

Subject Index

demographic similarities to participant and, 33
dress code for, 51
experienced, 34-35, 39, 44-45
field observations of, 91
fraud and, 93, 116-117
full-time versus part-time, 32
gender of, 33
getting to know other, 50
hiring, 27, 31-39
minimum qualifications, 34-35
monitoring performance of, 87-88
morale and, 94-95
number of, 31-32
participant experience with previous, 75
participant relationship with, 56-57, 117-118
paying, 23, 47, 93
personal interview with, 37-38
productivity of, 4
quality appraisal and, 90-94
quality control and, 115
race of, 33
rehiring veteran, 39
safety issues and, 15-16, 48-49
scheduling and, 36, 37-38
seasonal versus year-round, 32-33
study background and, 53-54
supervision of, 81-97
training, 42-61
training veteran, 44-45
Interviewer attributes, participation rates and, 72
Interviewer supervisors:
checking assessment materials, 101
hiring, 27, 30-31
training interviewers and, 43
Interview materials:
computerized tracking of, 87
cost of duplicating, 22-23
storage location, 48
training and, 43
Interview rooms, 18-20
Investigator, training done by, 43

Job applications, 29. *See also* Hiring
Job interview, 28-29
Job requirements, 47

Job schedules, management of, 2-3

Legal documents, 117
Legal obligations, 47-49
Life-threatening situations, 48
Listening skills, 58
Longitudinal studies:
continued cooperation and, 91
data files for, 107
data protection and, 104
in-house data collection and, 17
rehiring interviewers for, 39
retaining interviewers for, 32

Mail:
informing potential participants by, 72-73
maintaining contact with participants through, 74
Mailing costs, 15, 23
Mail-in questionnaire, costs of, 15
Males, listing of young adult, 70
Management:
data, 98-113
of research team, 1-3
Managerial skills, 17
Media contact, 12
Morale, supervision and, 94-95

Names, variety of, 77
Newsletters, staff morale and, 94-95

Observation, training costs and, 32. *See also* Field observations
Office staff, getting to know, 49-50
"Other" categories, coding, 101

Participant(s):
assessing interaction with, 91
availability of, 31
behavior of, 56-57
demographic similarities to interviewer, 33
ethical issues and, 47-49

About the Authors

Magda Stouthamer-Loeber is co-director of the Life History Studies Group at Western Psychiatric Institute and Clinic of the University of Pittsburgh Medical Center. An associate professor of psychiatry and psychology at the University of Pittsburgh, she has conducted several studies requiring data collection by interviewers in the field. Dr. Stouthamer-Loeber completed her M.A. degree in psychology in the Netherlands and received her doctorate in clinical psychology from Queen's University, Kingston, Ontario, Canada, in 1979. She spent five years as a research associate at the Oregon Social Learning Center in Eugene, Oregon, where she helped conduct a pilot study for a longitudinal study. From Oregon she moved to her current position in Pittsburgh. She is currently co-directing the Pittsburgh Youth Study, a ten-year longitudinal study of inner city boys. Throughout her career, she has been interested in the "nuts and bolts" of conducting high quality research in the area of the development of antisocial behavior.

Welmoet Bok van Kammen received her B.A. in the Netherlands and her Ph.D. from the Johns Hopkins University in Baltimore, Maryland, in 1977. Her first job related to longitudinal research was as research coordinator of the Schizophrenia Research Unit at the Highland Drive Veterans Administration Medical Center in Pittsburgh, Pennsylvania. From 1987 until the present, she has worked for the Pittsburgh Youth Study, University of Pittsburgh Medical Center, as program director. With Dr. Magda Stouthamer-Loeber, she is responsible for the day-to-day management of the project. She has been involved in a variety of studies dealing with relapse prediction in schizophrenia, psychological sequelae of war-related stress, and substance use in children and adolescents.